MW01101084

Skateboarding

TITLES IN THIS SERIES INCLUDE:

Baseball

Basketball

Car Racing

Cycling

Equestrian

Figure Skating

Football

Golf

Gymnastics

Ice Hockey

Skiing

Snowboarding

Soccer

Surfing

Swimming

Taekwondo

Volleyball

Skateboarding

LIZABETH CRAIG

LUCENT BOOKS

A part of Gale, Cengage Learning

GALE
CENGAGE Learning·

Farmington Hills, Mich • San Francisco • New York • Waterville, Maine
Meriden, Conn • Mason, Ohio • Chicago

LIBRARY OF CONGRESS CATALOGING-IN-PUBLICATION DATA

Craig, Lizabeth.
  Skateboarding / by Lizabeth Craig.
    pages cm. -- (Science behind sports)
  Includes bibliographical references and index.
  ISBN 978-1-4205-1211-3 (hardcover)
  1. Skateboarding--Juvenile literature. 2. Sports sciences--Juvenile literature.
I. Title.
  GV859.8.C74 2014
  796.22--dc23
                                                2014008778

Lucent Books
27500 Drake Rd
Farmington Hills MI 48331

ISBN-13: 978-1-4205-1211-3
ISBN-10: 1-4205-1211-0

Printed in the United States of America
1 2 3 4 5 6 7 18 17 16 15 14

CONTENTS

On March 21, 1970, Slovenian ski jumper Vinko Bogataj took a terrible fall while competing at the Ski-Flying World Championships in Oberstdorf, West Germany. Bogataj's pinwheeling crash was caught on tape by an ABC *Wide World of Sports* film crew and eventually became synonymous with "the agony of defeat" in competitive sporting. While many viewers were transfixed by the severity of Bogataj's accident, most were not aware of the biomechanical and environmental elements behind the skier's fall—heavy snow and wind conditions that made the ramp too fast and Bogataj's inability to maintain his center of gravity and slow himself down. Bogataj's accident illustrates that, no matter how mentally and physically prepared an athlete may be, scientific principles—such as momentum, gravity, friction, and aerodynamics—always have an impact on performance.

Lucent Books' Science Behind Sports series explores these and many more scientific principles behind some of the most popular team and individual sports, including baseball, hockey, gymnastics, wrestling, swimming, and skiing. Each volume in the series focuses on one sport or group of related sports. The volumes open with a brief look at the featured sport's origins, history, and changes, then move on to cover the biomechanics and physiology of playing, related health and medical concerns, and the causes and treatment of sports-related injuries.

In addition to learning about the arc behind a curve ball, the impact of centripetal force on a figure skater, or how water buoyancy helps swimmers, Science Behind Sports readers will also learn how exercise, training, warming up, and diet and nutrition directly relate to peak performance and enjoyment of the sport. Volumes may also cover why certain sports are popular, how sports function in the business world, and which hot sporting issues—sports doping and cheating, for example—are in the news.

Basic physical science concepts, such as acceleration, kinetics, torque, and velocity, are explained in an engaging and accessible manner. The full-color text is augmented by fact boxes, sidebars, photos, and detailed diagrams, charts, and graphs. In addition, a subject-specific glossary, bibliography, and index provide further tools for researching the sports and concepts discussed throughout Science Behind Sports.

CHAPTER 1

The Story of Skateboarding

The story of skateboarding as a sport is not a very long one. As American sports go, skateboarding is a relative newcomer, dating back only to the 1950s.

Very simply, "skateboarding" means riding on a narrow wooden board that has four wheels attached to the bottom, two near the front, and two near the back. Each pair of wheels is attached to the board with "trucks," which are like the axles on a car. The trucks allow the wheels to spin and give them steerability, similar to a car's wheels. The skateboard is moved forward by the push of the rider's foot or by gravity as it rolls down a slope. Sounds simple enough, but modern skateboarding is more than just a fun way to get from place to place. It has evolved into a complex sport with hundreds of trick moves. It has also developed its own culture, including language, clothing, music, and movies.

Skateboarding has its roots in surfing, an activity that was part of Polynesian and Hawaiian culture for centuries before it became a sport in America in the late 1800s when three Hawaiian princes came to San Mateo, California, to go to college and brought surfing with them. They rode the waves on boards made from the local redwood trees. The sport quickly caught on, and, by the late 1940s, surfing had become an extremely popular sport in California. Surfing movies were made, and surfing competitions were held.

Sidewalk Surfing

By the 1950s, many surfers had become so attached to the sport they felt the need to find some kind of similar activity they could do to maintain and improve their skills at times when the waves were low and surfing was not possible. At some point, someone (no one knows exactly who or exactly when) decided to take the handlebars off a child's homemade wooden scooter and ride it like a surfboard on land, and skateboarding was born. Surfers called this activity "sidewalk surfing." Soon, they began to build their own "sidewalk surfboards." For sidewalk surfing, the board was little more than a plank of wood with steel roller skate wheels nailed to the underside. The metal wheels made for a rough and dangerous ride and had very little traction on pavement. That meant the boards could slip and slide easily. The trucks were rigid, which gave the boards no turning or maneuvering ability. It was almost impossible to avoid obstacles such as stones, sticks, or cracks in the sidewalk. As rider Bob Schmidt described the ride, "It was wobblier than [heck], moved way too fast, and vibrated on the asphalt enough to jar every bone in your body and loosen every tooth. It was more like getting electrocuted than anything

Three boys ride on an early skateboard— roller skate wheels nailed to the bottom of a plank of wood—in 1944.

else."[1] Riders did not do any tricks at this time; it was only done as a substitute for "real" surfing. It was usually done barefoot, and the moves were similar to those done on a surfboard.

Throughout the 1950s, despite the rough ride, sidewalk surfing gained popularity, not only among surfers but among younger kids who had not yet learned to surf, and among kids in other parts of the country who didn't live near the ocean. In 1959, the first commercially manufactured skateboard was produced by the Roller Derby Company, a company founded in 1936 that made boots for ice skates and roller skates. The Roller Derby board was made of wood, and although it still had steel wheels, the trucks had been improved to make the board more steerable.

Skateboarding in the 1960s

Skateboarding gained even more popularity among surfers when Larry Stevenson, who, in 1961, was working for a surfing magazine called *Surf Guide*, noticed how many kids were riding boards and imitating surfers. He began writing articles about skateboarding and publishing them in *Surf Guide*. Surfing was continuing its explosive rise in popularity, and Stevenson's articles introduced skateboarding to a rapidly expanding surfing community.

The first specialty skate shop, the Val Surf Shop, opened in 1962 in North Hollywood, California. As skateboarding increased, several American manufacturers began mass-producing professional-quality skateboards, inspired by the shape and movement of surfboards. Stevenson started Makaha Skateboards in 1963 and sponsored the first skateboard competition at a junior high school in Hermosa, California, that year. He tried different materials for the board, such as plywood and foam, which were stronger and lighter in weight than solid wood. He tried making wheels out of nylon, a synthetic substance invented in 1934. Nylon was

OFF THE HOOK
More than 50%

The percentage of skateboarders in the United States who live in California.

more durable and dent-resistant than metal.

In 1964, Hobie Alter, a popular California surfboard maker, added skateboards to his business. That year he joined forces with Baron Hilton—owner of the Hilton Hotel chain and the San Diego Chargers football team—whose sons Dave and Steve were avid skateboarders. The Hobie company improved the strength of skateboards by producing pressure-molded boards made with thin layers of wood glued and pressed together. They also manufactured their own trucks instead of buying them from roller skate companies. To promote their skateboards, they put together a team of top skateboarders, including Dave Hilton. The team began experimenting with simple tricks. They traveled across the country, doing shows and demonstrating their skills. At one stop, more than ten thousand people showed up to watch. Other manufacturers also put teams together to promote their boards.

Patti McGee, an early skateboarding celebrity, does a handstand on her skateboard in 1965.

Television soon picked up on the skateboarding craze. Skateboarding teams performed on an early television show called *Surf's Up,* which helped promote skateboarding as an activity. In 1965, ABC's *Wide World of Sports* broadcast the National Skateboarding Championships in Anaheim, California. Patti McGee, an early skateboarding celebrity who was sponsored by Hobie, appeared on popular TV shows of the day such as *The Mike Douglas Show* and *The Tonight Show Starring Johnny Carson.* She also appeared on the cover of *Life* magazine, doing a handstand on her board.

Also in 1965, the first skateboarding magazine came out. *The Quarterly Skateboarder* was published by a surfing magazine publisher, and the cover showed Dave Hilton doing a high jump on a skateboard. In the magazine, its editor, John Severson, wrote:

Whenever a new sport comes into existence or an existing sport suddenly gains popularity, its thrills are often compared to other sports. People compare the thrills of surfing to sky diving, bullfighting, skiing, and other exciting individual-participation sports. These same comparisons are being made in the sport of skateboarding. . . . We predict a real future for the sport—a future that could go as far as the Olympics.[2]

All these promotions worked; Hobie, Makaha, and other manufacturers such as Jack's, Kip's, and Bing's, could barely keep up with demand. More than 50 million boards were sold in three years. By 1965, Makaha had sold more than $10 million in boards.

Skateboarding Hits a Slump

Severson and many others predicted great things for skateboarding, but they also knew that skateboarding as a sport was already facing a challenge. Severson wrote in *The*

Skateboarding and the Olympics

Discussions about skateboarding as an Olympic event have been ongoing for several decades. It has been controversial, however, with disagreement about whether or not it is even a sport at all. Some also may feel that skateboarding would lose its artistic and creative independence by being structured and regulated as an Olympic sport. Skateboard tricks are difficult to measure accurately, so fair judging standards might be a challenge as well. If skateboarding is to be recognized as an Olympic sport, it will have to overcome several major obstacles. First, according to the rules established by the International Olympic Committee (IOC), a sport must have a governing body, and, currently, skateboarding has none that is universally recognized. A sport must also be regulated by an international federation and adopt the Olympic charter. Even then, there is a long list of requirements to fulfill before the sport can be included. The IOC also requires organized world championship competitions, as well as national competitions held in at least seventy countries. Even with all of these challenges, skateboarding eventually may become an Olympic sport.

Quarterly Skateboarder in 1965, "The sport is being molded and we believe that doing the right thing now will lead to a bright future for the sport. Already there are storm clouds on the horizon with opponents of the sport talking about ban and restriction."[3] Safety was the issue. Some manufacturers were using wheels made out of clay, which was actually a compressed mixture of paper, plastic, and finely ground walnut shells. Clay wheels were cheaper to make, but they wore out easily. Worn-out clay wheels and dented steel wheels made falls very likely for all but the most experienced riders. As more people, especially younger kids, took up skateboarding, injuries became much more common and more severe. By the fall of 1965, parents and medical professionals were pressuring shops to stop selling skateboards. After several head injuries led to deaths, many cities across America banned skateboarding altogether. Almost overnight, the popularity of skateboarding evaporated. Skate shops closed, other stores stopped carrying skateboards, Christmas orders were cancelled, and manufacturers went out of business. *The Quarterly Skateboarder* stopped publication. Skateboarding as a sport entered what was to be the first of several slumps during its history.

Despite the sudden crash in skateboarding's popularity, people continued to skate, especially in California surfing communities. They went back to building their own boards—although parts were hard to find.

The 1970s: Skateboarding Makes a Comeback

A major improvement in skateboard design came in 1972 with the invention of wheels made of a new petroleum-based plastic called polyurethane, a very durable substance used in all kinds of products from car tires, to carpeting, to medical devices. In 1970, a young man named Frank Nasworthy visited a plastics factory called Creative

The invention of the polyurethane wheel by Frank Nasworthy was largely responsible for skateboarding's comeback by 1975.

Urethane owned by a friend's father. The factory had tried making roller skate wheels out of polyurethane because it provided better traction on hard surfaces. Better traction, however, meant a slower ride, and roller skaters preferred the faster ride that metal wheels provided. Nasworthy tried the plastic wheels on his own skateboard and discovered that they provided a much smoother ride on rough pavement than either clay or metal wheels.

When Nasworthy moved to California in 1971 to surf, he noticed the large number of people who were skateboarding. He still believed that polyurethane might make a good material for skateboard wheels, even though they were slower. He believed that the improved traction and smoother ride would make skateboarding more fun and a lot safer. "I thought if I could sell one set of wheels to each surfing shop," he said, "I could make some money and surf at the same time."[4] In 1972, with only $700, he started a company called Cadillac Wheels. He sold his wheels to surf shops all over California, and boards made with them quickly became high-demand items by skateboarders. "The word spread fast," he remembers. "The next month kids were coming down from L.A. Then it all just went wild."[5] In 1973 alone, "Captain Cadillac," as he had come to be known, sold ten thousand sets of polyurethane wheels, and, in 1975, sales topped three hundred thousand sets.

By 1975, largely due to Nasworthy's new wheels, skateboarding had made a comeback. New manufacturers opened, many of them making trucks especially designed for skateboards rather than for roller skates. That year, a new skateboarding magazine called *Skateboarder* started publication. Also in 1975, one of the largest skateboarding competitions since the 1960s, the Del Mar Nationals, was held in Del Mar, California, with more than five hundred contestants. At the competition, a team of twelve riders from Santa Monica, California, introduced a new style of low, smooth skateboarding, based on Hawaiian surfing. They were called the Zephyr Team, or Z-Boys, and they became one of the most famous and influential teams in the sport. Skateboarding now had "stars" such as Stacy Peralta, Jay Adams, and Tony Alva.

Skateboarders, hungry for new places to skate and new challenges to their skills, brought their boards to places such as parking lots, cement drainage ditches, and empty reservoirs. Some cities decided they did not want kids skateboarding in such places because it led to a lot of trespassing. They knew they could not stop the activity, however, so they began to build skate parks specifically designed for skateboarding, with various kinds of surface shapes such as cement bowls, ramps, and half-pipes. The first skate parks appeared in Port Orange, Florida, and San Diego County, California, in 1976. Many more soon followed.

New Tricks and Another Slump

In the mid-1970s, improvements in skateboard design were coming rapidly. Lighter and stronger materials such as fiberglass and aluminum were used for making the boards, but wooden boards were still the most common. Improved truck design, along with Nasworthy's polyurethane wheels, made skateboards much more maneuverable. In 1969, Stevenson had patented his invention of the kicktail—the upward curve at the end of the skateboard that is used for almost all skateboarding tricks. As a result, many skateboarders began experimenting with more complex and challenging moves.

A skateboarder practices vert skating in a Claremont, California, storm drain in 1975.

One 1970s innovation in skateboarding was "vert" skating. Vert skating means riding the skateboard on vertical surfaces rather than just downhill or on flat ground. It was made possible largely due to the improved grip of Nasworthy's new wheels. It also coincided with an environmental crisis that happened in 1976. That year, a severe drought hit California. Many swimming pools lay drained and empty during the drought, and skateboarders soon discovered that the curved bottoms of empty pools were a great place to ride their boards. They learned to ride up and down the vertical part of the pool walls, and vert skating was born. Boards made just for vert skating were 2 to 3 inches (5 to 7cm) wider than regular boards, and provided better stability on vertical surfaces. Many skateboarders began to devote most of their skating time to vert skating. Vert stars such as Peralta, Adams, and Alva became famous almost overnight. Others preferred to continue freestyle skating in public areas and in skate parks.

In 1978, another new trick revolutionized skateboarding. It was called the "ollie," named after its inventor, Alan "Ollie" Gelfand. In 1977, while on a skateboarding tour, pro skater Peralta saw the fourteen-year-old Gelfand skate up the side of a bowl and over the lip of the bowl, "catching air" while maintaining control of the board with his feet. He appeared to be defying gravity with the move, and Peralta was fascinated. Later pro skaters such as Rodney Mullen adapted the move for skating on the ground. The ollie allows a skateboarder to lift his board off the ground while riding by slamming the rear kicktail down, which raises the front end off the ground. The ollie allows the rider to jump onto and over obstacles, and has become the foundation move for hundreds of other tricks and trick combinations.

Near the end of the 1970s, skateboarding as a sport experienced another slump, again having to do with its hazardous

The Zephyr Team

In 1972, the same year that Frank Nasworthy introduced his polyurethane skateboard wheels, a trio of surfers named Jeff Ho, Craig Stecyk, and Skip Engblom opened a surf shop called Jeff Ho and Zephyr Surfboard Productions, in a rundown section of west Los Angeles, California, called Dogtown. Dogtown was full of young surfers who had little else in their lives except surfing and who were very protective of their surfing territory. They had a reputation for being aggressive, antisocial misfits, but they were a close-knit group who respected performance and skill.

The Zephyr surf shop formed a surfing team called the Zephyr Team, and the Z-Boys, as they were called, used skateboarding as something to do when they could not surf. Soon, skateboarding became a way to express themselves athletically and creatively. They rode their skateboards low, with knees bent way down, as if they were surfing, sometimes dragging their fingers along the pavement the way they would along a wave. In 1975 the team entered the Del Mar Nationals competition and fascinated the crowd with their fearless style of riding. When *Skateboarder* magazine launched in 1975, Craig Stecyk wrote a series of articles called the *Dogtown Articles*, drawing even more attention to the team and to skateboarding. Several months later, the team fell victim to the fame and fortune they had earned. The huge amounts of money being offered to them by big skateboard companies made it difficult for the team to stay together, and they disbanded. By that time, however, the team of misfits from Dogtown had changed skateboarding forever. Their story was chronicled in the 2005 movie *Lords of Dogtown*.

nature. New, more complex tricks and vert skating were causing increasing numbers of injuries at skate parks, especially at those where the surfaces were not properly maintained. By 1980, as liability insurance rates rose and fewer people came to the parks, most parks were forced to close.

The 1980s: Skateboarding Goes Underground

With skate parks closed and private property areas off-limits, some skateboarders resorted to building their own plywood skate ramps in their backyards or in vacant lots. Many others took to the streets, and learned to skate on the tops of low walls, steps of buildings, and handrails. Street, or freestyle, skating became very popular among diehard skateboarders, and street stars such as Mark Gonzales and Mike Vallely became well-known. At this time, freestyle and vert skating diverged into two different skating disciplines, each with their own followers, stars, and fans.

During the 1980s, skateboarding experienced a short upsurge. Several skateboard companies were started by older pro skaters who were no longer skating competitively. These companies continued to improve on board and truck design. Skaters such as Mullen continued to create even more complex tricks and stunts such as kickflips and pop shuvits, with the ollie as the basis for most of them. They discovered that smaller, harder wheels helped them get more height, or "pop," on their ollies. Movies about skating and skateboarders were made, such as *Thrashin'* (1986), *The Search for Animal Chin* (1987), and *Gleaming the Cube* (1989).

Once again, however, at the end of the 1980s and in the early 1990s, skateboarding went into yet another slump. Vert skating began to lose popularity, and most skaters returned to street skating. Professional vert skaters such as Tony Hawk suffered financially and emotionally as their brand of the sport declined.

OFF THE HOOK

247

The *Guinness World Records* number of consecutive ollies performed by eighteen-year-old Eric Carlin in 2011.

Another Resurgence

Each time skateboarding became unpopular, it always seemed to bounce back, and each of these slumps was a little less severe than the one before. In the mid-1990s, the sport started yet another recovery. This time, however, skateboarding looked a little different—more edgy and more rebellious. This was the era of punk rock and grunge, and skating and skateboarders took on the image of the

Tony Hawk

Tony Hawk is widely regarded as one of the best vert skateboarders in the history of the sport. He was born on May 12, 1968, in Carlsbad, California. He got his first skateboard at age nine, and by twelve he was winning amateur competitions throughout California. He turned professional at fourteen, and, by sixteen, he had already earned a reputation as one of the world's best skaters. By the time he graduated from high school, he had earned enough from winnings and endorsements to buy his first house. By twenty-five, he had won or finished second in 92 of the 103 competitions he entered, and was named vert skating's world champion twelve years in a row.

In 1991, when vert skating experienced its crash in popularity, his income shrank drastically, but he did not give up on the sport. He opened his own skateboard company called Birdhouse Projects. At first, it did not do very well. Later in the 1990s, however, when skateboarding rebounded, the company took off. He added a line of skateboarding clothing for kids called Hawk Clothing, and, in 1999, he launched Tony Hawk's Pro Skater Videogames. At that year's X Games, he became the first to land a "900," turning his board 900 degrees (two and a half turns) in midair. Later that year, he retired from competition, but he still runs exhibition tours and appears in movies and on television. His Tony Hawk Foundation supports the building of skate parks in underprivileged areas all over the United States.

An eighteen-year-old Tony Hawk performs his vert skating in 1986.

poor, angry, skater punk. Skateboarding and skaters were considered an underground element of society. Many people considered skaters to be little more than an antisocial subculture of criminal types. This negative image appealed to a lot of young people at the time, however, and helped fuel skateboarding's popularity.

In 1995, ESPN held the first Extreme Games, or X Games, in Rhode Island. The competition included skateboarding along with other "extreme" sports. With skateboarding now being televised on a respected sports network, skateboarding began to reenter the mainstream and became more acceptable to the general public. The X Games also brought about a renewal of interest in vert skating among both skaters and sports fans.

Since 2000, skateboarding has continued to become more of a mainstream activity. Video games, movies, toys, and skateboards for children have helped dispel the notion of skateboarders as punks or criminals. New boards are much safer, and protective equipment is more effective. New skate parks have been built all over the country to help get skaters off the streets and into a safer environment. The increase in skate parks is also helping vert skating make a comeback. Skateboarding is being used in physical education programs to encourage school attendance and build confidence, self-expression, and self-discipline. There has been discussion among skaters, skateboard organizations, and the International Olympic Committee about making skateboarding an Olympic event. Professional skaters, such as Geoff Rowley, Bucky Lasek, and Vanessa Torres, are sponsored by companies such as Vans, Mountain Dew, Element, and Monster, and can earn thousands of dollars a month in competition winnings, public appearances, and company salaries.

Meanwhile, skateboarding continues to evolve, with new tricks and stunts being created almost every day. Clothing especially designed for skaters is a huge industry. Protective gear continues to improve in quality and safety. The skateboard itself continues to evolve as well, and it has come a long way from the old wooden scooter with roller skate wheels on the bottom, to the modern, high-tech piece of sports equipment it is today.

CHAPTER 2

The Science of Skateboard Design

The skateboard itself has a longer history than its sport. What started out as a simple wooden plank with steel roller skate wheels has evolved into a sleek, balanced, high-tech piece of sporting equipment, highly engineered and made from natural and modern synthetic materials. Over the decades, as skateboarding has gone through its ups and downs in popularity, and as riding styles have changed, skateboards have changed in size, shape, and materials to fit the times and the needs of skaters. The design of modern boards makes possible the creation of intricate tricks and gravity-defying stunts that make skateboarding so much fun to watch and so thrilling to do.

The Very Beginning

Today's skateboards have several "ancestors," dating back to the 1920s and 1930s. At that time, children built homemade scooters. The scooters were made from a plank or a two-by-four with roller skate wheels attached to the bottom. A wooden fruit crate or milk box was attached to the front. Sometimes, handles were nailed to the top of it. The rider would stand on the plank, hold on to the handles and push the scooter forward with one foot. When he sped up enough, or if he was going downhill, he could put both feet on the board and ride the scooter. Another kind of scooter had three large wheels and a circular handle like a steering wheel. It was propelled by pumping the movable deck with a seesaw action. Children during this time also attached skate wheels to pieces of wood and sat on them sideways, holding on to the ends and holding their legs up off the ground.

In the 1940s, the four-wheeled Skeeter, or Skeeter Skate, appeared. It was similar to a skateboard and was made out of aluminum. The Skeeter had removable handles. It also had axles attached to the wheels that allowed it to be steered.

Sidewalk surfing, with a converted scooter, was the trend of the 1950s when surfing became so popular that surfers invented a way to do it on land when conditions at sea were not conducive.

Today's skateboard, however, is much more than just a board with wheels. It has several parts that all work closely together to provide precision performance, speed, and maneuverability. Each part has a very important role in making skateboarding the creative, complex activity that it is. Basically, a skateboard consists of three main parts: the board, also called the deck; a set of trucks; and a set of wheels. Each of these main parts includes other parts that allow it to function at its best.

The Deck

The deck is the board that the rider stands on. Most skateboard decks are made of seven to nine thin layers of wood, called veneers. The veneers are usually made of maple wood because it is a hard wood and resists breaking. Other materials have been used as well, such as bamboo or aluminum, but maple is the material of choice for most manufacturers. According to skateboard designer Tim Piumarta, "With all the alternate materials we've tried, from epoxy and fiberglass to carbon loaded thermoplastic nylon, nothing has had the combination of toughness, elasticity, feel and response of laminated sugar maple wood."[6]

The veneers are glued together using special adhesives called laminates. They are then put into a machine called a press and pressed together very tightly to fuse them into a

solid piece. As many as three to five boards can be put into the press at once. They are left in the press for thirty minutes to one hour. The press also molds the board into the characteristic curved shape of a skateboard deck. After the veneers are pressed and molded, the board is cut into shape, and holes are drilled to attach the wheels. Finally, the deck is sanded, painted, and finished with a layer of a protective sealant.

A skateboard deck has two shape features. The first is called the concave. The concave refers to the three-dimensional curves that are in a skateboard at the sides, the front, and the back. Most modern skateboard decks are slightly higher on the sides than in the middle. Many riders feel this shape gives them better control of the board, especially when performing tricks. The "nose," or front end of the board, and the "tail," or back end, are angled upward slightly, which also helps the rider control the board during tricks. The raised ends are called kicktails. The nose kicktail is usually slightly wider than the tail kicktail. The concave and the kicktails are shaped when the board is in the press.

A variety of skateboard decks are on display at the 2013 Venice Beach Surf and Skate Festival in California.

Some boards are more concave than others, depending on the manufacturer.

The second shape is the called the plan form. This is simply the shape of the outline of the board. Skateboards are made in a variety of plan forms. They may be oval, rectangular,

ANATOMY OF A SKATEBOARD

A basic skateboard deck is made by molding a stack of thin wood veneer layers in a press. It's all held together with strong epoxy and other glues. Some skateboards also use fiberglass and other materials.

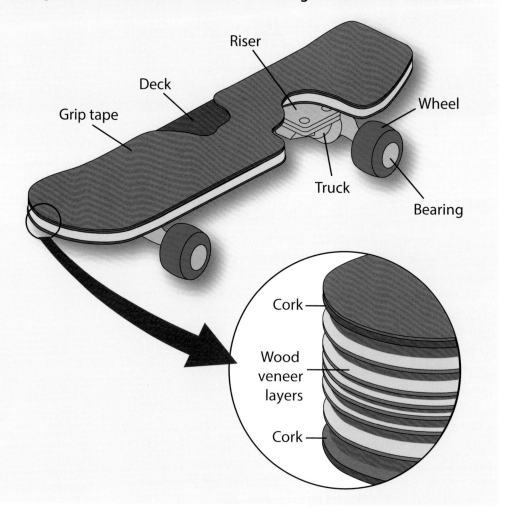

Riser

Deck

Grip tape

Wheel

Truck

Bearing

Cork

Wood veneer layers

Cork

pointed at the ends, or shaped like a surfboard. They may have one rounded end and one square end. Some have cutout areas at the front and back so that the wheels are visible. The shape a rider chooses depends on the kind of riding he likes to do.

Most skateboard decks measure about 7 to 8 inches (18 to 20cm) wide, about 32 inches (81cm) long, and about ½ inch (1cm) thick. The width and length also vary, however, according to the preferred style of riding. For example, boards made for vert skating are generally wider than those used for street skating, and riders who want more speed may use longer boards.

Attached to the top surface of the deck is a piece of grip tape. Grip tape, as the name implies, improves the rider's grip on the board by helping to prevent his feet from slipping. It can also be used by the rider to flip or spin the board in the air, if he drags his feet along the tape. Grip tape looks and feels like sandpaper and comes in several colors. It has an adhesive backing that attaches it to the deck. It can be attached in one big piece, in strips, or in pieces cut into intricate shapes for a custom look.

The Trucks

Trucks are aluminum parts attached to the front and back ends of the underside of the board that hold the wheels and allow the board to be steered. When a rider shifts his weight on the board by leaning to the right or the left, the trucks pivot and allow the wheels to turn in the direction of the lean. It is similar to turning the steering wheel in a car to make its wheels turn. The distance between the two trucks is called the wheelbase. A longer wheelbase increases stability. A shorter wheelbase increases maneuverability but is less stable.

Trucks are made up of several parts. The baseplate is the part that is bolted to the underside of the deck. The hanger

OFF THE HOOK
300 psi

The pressure, in pounds per square inch, exerted on the skateboard while in the press machine.

is a triangular-shaped part that extends down from the baseplate and attaches to it at a joint called the pivot point, or pivot cup. The hanger also holds the axle. The skateboard wheels are attached to the ends of the axle. The kingpin is a large bolt that runs down through the baseplate and into the hanger. Urethane discs, called bushings, are placed around the kingpin on either side of the hanger to help keep the hanger and the baseplate together. There is also a bushing holding the hanger and the baseplate together at the pivot point.

A nut on the kingpin can be used to tighten the kingpin bushings. The tighter the bushings, the more stable the skateboard is but the harder it is to turn it while riding. Looser bushings allow for a looser truck and quicker

Choosing the Right Skateboard

When it comes to choosing a skateboard, it is important for the rider to choose the right size and shape for his or her height, weight, foot size, and skill level. A skateboard sizing chart helps a rider determine which length is best for his height. Longer boards are difficult for shorter riders to control, so they should choose a shorter board. As they grow taller, however, they may need to trade in the short board for a longer one that is more comfortable and easier to control. Heavier riders should choose a wider, heavier deck that provides adequate support. Wider trucks made of alloy steel are also a good choice for heavier riders, along with larger, harder wheels. Riders with larger feet may also need a wider board that they can move around on more comfortably and safely.

Beginners also may want a wider board that has more stability, is easier to control, and makes it easier to develop balance—decreasing the likelihood of falling. Flat boards or boards with lower kicks at the ends are also easier for beginners to control, while boards with higher kicks have more "pop" and help experienced riders perform higher flips and jumps.

The type of board chosen also depends on what kinds of moves the rider wants to do. Wider boards, around 8 inches (20cm), are better for vert skating and for skate parks. Narrower boards are better for street skating. They are also better for doing tricks because narrower boards are easier to pop for aerial tricks. For just getting from place to place, the longer, wider longboard is ideal.

turns, but make the skateboard less stable, especially at high speeds.

Risers are thin blocks or pads that fit between the truck baseplate and the deck. They are usually about ¼- to ⅜-inch thick (6.35mm to 9.52mm). They increase the distance between the deck and the ground, which many riders feel gives the board more "pop" when doing tricks. They also create more distance between the deck and larger wheels to help prevent the wheels from hitting the bottom of the deck during sharp turns. This is called "wheel bite" and can cause the board to skid or stop suddenly and lead to a fall. Risers also help with shock absorption.

Fausto Vitello, designer of the popular Independent brand truck, says:

> The basic skateboard truck has not changed in probably fifty or sixty years. It was designed around the 1920s for ballroom roller-skate dancing. . . . The basic system for allowing a truck to turn is called the Chicago pivot, and all modern trucks are derived from that. What has changed in the Chicago Pivot truck is

A variety of trucks can be seen on the skateboards of kids waiting their turn at the Nathan Lazarus Skatepark in Nederland, Colorado.

that we have refined the system to allow better turning, more stability, and certain other features that skaters demand.[7]

He also says that any design changes in trucks have to be made with the needs of the rider in mind. "When we design skateboard trucks," he says, "the most important part of the process is the input we get from the actual riders. We can't design what we think is an improvement without having their input. The ultimate test is what skateboarders say about it."[8]

The Wheels

Just as there are different kinds of decks for different kinds of skateboarding, there are different types of wheels as well. Some work better on rough terrain; some are better for smoother surfaces. Vert skating and street skating need different wheels for maximum performance. Skateboard wheels vary according to size and the hardness of the material out of which they are made.

The original skateboard wheels were simply steel roller skate wheels nailed to the underside of a board. They had very little traction, slipped on the ground easily, and provided a very rough ride. The 1960s clay wheels were cheaper than steel, and provided a slightly smoother ride than steel, but they still did not provide very good traction on pavement. They also wore out very quickly; downhill slalom skaters could go through a set of clay wheels in one day of riding. The invention of the polyurethane wheel by Frank Nasworthy in 1972 revolutionized skateboarding by providing good traction, durability, and a smooth ride on pavement.

The size of a skateboard wheel is measured by its diameter, or height, in millimeters (mm). The diameter determines how tall the wheel is. The average skateboard wheel, for general skating, measures from about 52 to 55mm across (about 2.05 to 2.2 inches). For more technical trick skating, a shorter wheel of 45 to 55mm (about 1.8 to 2.1 inches) is better for landing ollies and performing other tricks because a shorter wheel holds the board closer to the ground and makes it more maneuverable. Vert skaters may choose larger wheels from 55 to 65mm (2.1 to 2.6 inches). Larger wheels are better for vert skating on ramps because they provide the speed necessary for getting up to the lip of the ramp. Larger wheels roll faster because one revolution, or turn, of a larger wheel covers more ground than one revolution of a smaller wheel. For this reason, people who like to cover long distances on their skateboards (cruisers)

Polyurethane

Polyurethane is a strong, flexible synthetic substance used in thousands of products—from toys to airplanes, couch cushions to medical supplies. It is used to seal and protect surfaces, as an adhesive, or as insulation. Polyurethane was invented in the late 1930s in Germany. It was used as an aircraft coating during World War II. Throughout the 1940s and 1950s, scientists in Europe and the United States developed and improved it with different combinations of molecules, creating rigid and semirigid foams as well as many other forms for many uses.

Chemically, the polyurethane molecule is called a polymer. A polymer is a molecule made up of a chain of smaller molecules called monomers. The monomers are chemically bonded in a process called polymerization. The main monomers in polyurethane are isocyanates and polyols. Depending on the particular combinations of monomers used, polyurethane can be hard and solid, rubbery and flexible, foamy, or liquid. Polyurethane that is semirigid but still somewhat flexible is called an elastomer. This is the kind that skateboard wheels are made of because it is shock-absorbing but still durable enough to keep its shape.

Although the two terms are often used interchangeably, polyurethane is not the same as urethane, also called ethyl carbamate. Urethanes are single-molecule compounds used in products such as insecticides, medicines, paints, varnishes, and solvents. Urethanes are not as tough or hard as polyurethanes. They are also more toxic to people and animals than polyurethanes and can cause cancer in animals. In people, exposure to high levels of urethanes can cause kidney and liver damage, coma, and bleeding; it has not been proven to cause cancer.

OFF THE HOOK

25A

The durometer of a typical rubber band.

like even larger wheels—up to 75mm in diameter (almost 3 inches).

Another important feature of skateboard wheels is the hardness of the wheel, called its durometer. A wheel is given a numerical durometer designation based on its measured hardness using a scale that includes a number and a letter. The higher the number, the harder the wheel. Most skateboard wheels are measured using the "A" scale. For example, a medium-grade hardness would be designated as 98A or 99A. Street skaters may choose a harder wheel, up to 101A, because harder wheels roll faster and are more durable on rough surfaces. Vert skaters also like harder wheels for their better speed and smooth ride on ramps and bowls. Cruisers, on the other hand, choose softer wheels, in the 75A to 85A range, because they provide better traction on rougher surfaces. Some wheels have two durometers—one for the outer part of the wheel, and one for a harder, inner layer around the center core, where most of the stress on the wheel is located. "B" and "D" scales are used for dual-durometer wheels. A regular 99A wheel is about equivalent in hardness to an 82B or a 45D dual-durometer wheel.

A third feature of wheels, which many people may not consider, is the color of the wheel. Color makes a difference because the more color, or dye, that is put into a wheel, the less room there is for the polyurethane molecules that give it strength. Dye in the wheels, therefore, causes the wheel to be less durable, which makes it more likely to wear out and get flat spots. The highest-performing skateboard wheels are clear or whitish in color.

Bearings are small parts in the center of the skateboard wheel that allow it to turn smoothly on its axle. Bearings are the least durable part of the skateboard because bearings were originally designed for use in machines. They were not really designed to handle the side-to-side stresses and impact forces that skateboarding places on them. There is one bearing on each side of each wheel, for a total of eight bearings on a skateboard. Although wheels vary in size, bearings

Colorful skateboard wheels look good but are less durable than clear or whitish ones.

are one universal size and fit into wheels of all sizes. Each bearing contains six to eight balls, called ball bearings. The ball bearings are located between two circular tracks called races. There is an outer race and a smaller inner race. They are held in place and separated from each other by a ring called a Delrin Crown, which looks very much like a king's crown. The ball bearings in their crowns are protected by a bearing shield, which keeps dirt out and keeps the bearings inside the crown. The whole assembly is housed inside a protective metal casing.

Longboards

A longboard, as the name implies, is a board that is longer and wider than a traditional skateboard. Like skateboards, longboards vary by length, shape, and wheel choice depending on their intended use. Longboards typically range from 40 to 60 inches (102 to 152cm) in length, but can be as long as 80 inches (203cm). Decks may be flat or concave. They may have cutout areas at the front and back to prevent wheel bite. Some have "drop" decks, in which the foot platform is lower than the truck mountings, which gives it more stability but less traction. Others have "drop through" decks, with their mounting plate on the top of the deck and hangers that extend down through the deck, also providing stability. Some longboards combine the two. Longboards usually have larger, wider wheels than skateboards, which gives them a smoother, faster ride and simulates the feeling of surfing.

Skateboard Maintenance

Skateboards are carefully designed and engineered to provide the best possible ride. Proper care and maintenance are necessary in order to extend the life of the skateboard and for the user to experience a safe and enjoyable ride. The parts of the board most often replaced are the deck, the kingpins, and the bearings.

Grip tape is essential for proper control of the board and should be replaced when it gets worn or frayed. It should also be cleaned if it gets dirty or muddy. Grip gum is a product that looks like an eraser and will clean most of the dirt off the grip tape. The board should not be exposed to moisture or to large fluctuations in temperature. This can weaken the wood and cause it to warp or break. The bolts that hold the trucks to the deck will loosen over time and must be kept tight to prevent cracks and breakage, and to prevent the wheels from falling off.

Trucks and wheels need to be checked for cracks and loose axle nuts. Wheels should be rotated, like the tires on a car, so that they wear evenly. Bearings should be kept clean and well lubricated for best spin. Some bearing brands have shields that can be removed for cleaning and lubricating. For the most part, however, they should not be taken out because the prying action of removing them can alter the shape of the wheel so that the bearing will not fit as tightly once it is reinserted.

They may have softer wheels for better traction on rough terrain, although the softer wheels will decrease speed.

The most common use for longboards is travel. Their greater size and weight give them more momentum, which means they go farther with each push of the rider's foot. This makes them well suited for covering greater distances with less effort. They are designed with looser trucks for easier turning. They may have kicktails on them to help lift the front of the board for getting on and off curbs. Land paddling is a way to travel on a longboard using a pole or stick to propel the board down the road. The stick can also be used for balance and to help slow down the board.

Longboards may be used for downhill riding or racing, in which the object is to go as fast as possible without losing control of the board. A popular form of downhill racing is the slalom, which involves riding the board on a zigzag course, weaving in and out of a line of poles or cones. Slalom boards vary from 40 to 50 inches (102 to 127cm), with shorter boards used for courses with sharper turns, and longer boards for steeper courses with larger turns. They have softer wheels for better grip in the turns. Another kind of downhill board is the buttboard, which requires the rider

Longboards are great for travel because the larger size and weight gives them more momentum with each push.

to sit on the board while riding and to control the speed with his feet.

Longboarders can also use their boards for trick riding, but the extra size and weight requires a great deal of skill and strength to control them through tricks. A longboard rider may use Sky Hooks, which are brackets attached to the deck of the board that hold the rider's feet firmly on the board. Sky Hooks help the downhill rider stay on the board at high speeds, help the slalom rider maneuver his board through tight turns, and allow the trick rider to move his board without having to grip it with his hands.

Mountainboards

Mountainboards, also called dirtboards or all-terrain boards, are more similar to snowboards than skateboards. Whereas skateboards were created because surfers wanted something similar to do in the winter, mountainboards were created because snowboarders wanted something similar to do in the summer. In 1978, on a bet, skateboarder Mike Motta attempted to skate down a Massachusetts hill on a regular skateboard. It did not go well. Something completely new was needed. The first real dirtboards appeared in 1989, and the term "mountainboarding" was coined in 1992. The first mountainboarding competition was held the following year.

Like skateboards, mountainboards are ridden on land, but they are not used on paved surfaces. They are the mountain bikes of the boarding world. Mountainboarders ride on gravel roads, down hillsides, in the woods, on mountain bike trails, BMX courses, and on dry boardercross (snowboarding competition) tracks. Also like skateboards, they have a deck and two sets of trucks. Instead of wheels, however, mountainboards have rubber tires mounted on plastic or metal wheels. They also have bindings, like snowboards, to secure the rider's feet to the board. Mountainboard decks are generally about 41 to 50 inches (104 to 127cm) long. They are made of carbon fiber, or of veneers of wood glued and pressed together like a skateboard. They vary by size, weight, shape, and flexibility according to the rider's preferences. They are angled up at the nose and tail like a skateboard, but for a different reason. The curves allow the center of the board to be lower to the ground, which provides more stability for the rider. Their aluminum trucks are similar to skateboard trucks except that they are sturdier and have longer axles. They also include shock absorbers, and springs, which help return the board to its centered position after a turn.

Mountainboard wheels range from 8 to 13 inches (20 to 33cm) in diameter. Smaller wheels are better for freestyle riding; larger wheels are better for speed and stability in downhill riding. The rubber air-filled tires mounted to the wheels vary in thickness. Some are two-ply, with two layers, others are four-ply. They have treads, like a car tire, for traction. Mountainboards, which are used for fast downhill riding, may also have brakes attached to the front wheels. The brakes are operated with a handheld lever, similar to a bicycle brake.

Mountainboards have rubber wheels and adjustable straps that hold the rider's feet on the board, to allow travel over varying terrains.

In the future, skateboards will continue to evolve in terms of their design and construction. "Technology will impact skateboards in the same way that it's hitting so many other products," says Brad Jakes, writer and skating enthusiast.

Stronger, lighter materials will appear and the rapid distribution of information means that board and truck design will advance even faster. . . . Maple is still the premium construction material for decks but surely the day is approaching when maple will be superseded, at least for some styles of board. New styles of boards will continue to emerge—the humble skateboard of the early days has already evolved into longboards, cruisers, retro boards, pool boards, old school, and mountain boards. As well as lighter, stronger trucks and better quality wheels, there'll be new deck plan shapes and original artwork.[9]

CHAPTER **3**

The Physics of Skateboarding

"In the beginning, skateboarding was simple. With nothing more than a two-by-four on roller-skate wheels, the sidewalk surfers of the 30s, 40s, and 50s had a straightforward mission: start at the top of a hill and ride down," says science writer Pearl Tesler. He goes on to say that: "The primary goal was just to stay on and avoid collisions; given the humble equipment and rough road conditions, it was no small challenge. Now, thanks in part to improvements in design and materials, skateboarders have a higher calling."[10]

Skateboarding looks simple enough: A rider pushes his foot against the ground, and the skateboard goes forward. That part is pretty simple, but what determines how fast and how far the board will go with one push? What is happening when the skater and his skateboard leave the ground and seem to defy gravity? How does a rider make his board do all those tricks? The answers lie in the study of physics. Physics is the branch of science that studies the relationships between matter, energy, time, and motion. It looks at the way physical forces such as gravity, friction, and momentum act on objects as they move. Physics plays a major role in every sport, including skateboarding.

Isaac Newton and Skateboarding

Several of the most basic concepts of physics were developed back in the 1600s by British scientist and mathematician Sir Isaac Newton (1643–1727). Best known for his ideas about gravity, Newton made many observations about other physical forces at work in nature, such as light and motion, and how these forces work together. Based on his observations, he developed three laws of motion. Skateboarding involves almost constant motion, whether on the ground or in the air, so all three of Newton's laws of motion relate to skateboarding.

Newton's first law of motion is the simplest of the three. It is called the Law of Inertia. In physics, "inertia" means that objects resist changes in the speed or direction of their motion. The law has two parts, each of which describes one kind of inertia. The first part describes static (not moving) inertia. Static inertia means that an object at rest will remain at rest unless it is acted upon by an outside force, and the force must be unbalanced, or, in other words, greater in

The harder a skateboarder pushes off, the faster and farther the board will go, demonstrating Newton's Law of Acceleration.

OFF THE HOOK

54 pounds (24kg)

What a skateboard of 2 lbs. (.9kg) would weigh on the sun.

one direction than the other. For example, a skateboard at rest on the ground will only move if someone or something pushes on it (the outside force). If two people push on it from opposite sides with equal force, the force is balanced, and so the board will not move. The second part of the Law of Inertia describes dynamic inertia. Dynamic inertia means that a moving object will continue to move at the same speed and in the same direction unless it is acted upon by a force that makes it stop or change direction. The pushed skateboard will continue to roll forward until air and ground resistance, or an obstacle such as a wall or someone's foot (the outside force), makes it stop.

Newton's second law is called the Law of Acceleration. This law says that the speed of a moving object depends on its mass and on how much force is applied to it. This law is expressed with a simple mathematical equation: $F = M \times A$, or Force equals Mass times Acceleration. It means several things. First, it means that an object will move faster and go farther the more force is applied to it. For example, the harder a skateboarder pushes off with his foot, the faster and farther the board will go. Second, it means that an object that has more mass needs more force to make it move at a particular speed. A heavier skateboard needs a stronger push to make it go at a certain speed. Third, it means that if two objects of different mass are acted upon by the same amount of force, the object with less mass will go faster. Using the same amount of force, a rider will move faster on a lighter skateboard than he will on a heavier one.

The third law of motion is called the Law of Action and Reaction, or the Law of Force Pairs. It says that for every action, there is an equal and opposite reaction. This means that whenever a force is applied to an object in one direction, an equal amount of force is applied in the opposite direction. The greater the force of the action, the greater will be the force of the reaction. There are many examples of this in nature. When a frog jumps off a lily pad, he moves

NEWTON'S LAWS OF MOTION AND SKATEBOARDING

Second Law: Force is equal to mass times acceleration.

The skateboard accelerates when a force acts on the combined mass of the skateboard and rider. The greater the mass, the greater the amount of force needed.

small mass:
large acceleration

large mass:
small acceleration

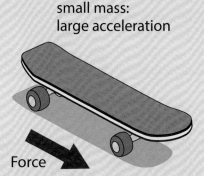

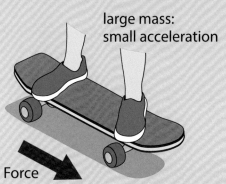

Force

Force

Third Law: Every action has an equal and opposite reaction.

When a skateboarder steps forward off the board, the board slips backward.

Action

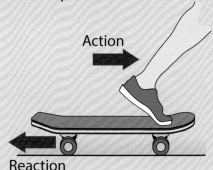

Reaction

As a skateboarder pushes and applies force on the ground, the ground pushes back with the same amount of force, and the board moves forward.

Action

Reaction

OFF THE HOOK

45 in. (114cm)

The highest recorded ollie—about the height of a mailbox.

forward (action) and the lily pad moves backward (opposite reaction). A fish must push water backward with its fins (action) in order to move himself forward (opposite reaction). If a skateboarder wants to move forward on his board (action), he must push backward on the ground (opposite reaction).

Newton's three laws of motion help illustrate what happens to a skateboard and its rider when the skateboarder is traveling in a straight line on a flat surface. Of course, there is a lot more to skateboarding than just moving in a straight line. There are hundreds of different skateboarding tricks that involve flips and turns, spins and leaps, all done at top speed. It can seem to the observer watching a competitor fly into the air and land safely that he is defying the laws of physics. Actually, however, he is using the laws of physics to his advantage. There are several concepts of physics that relate directly to skateboard tricks.

Gravity

Newton is also responsible for much of what we know about gravity. He defined gravity as a downward force that exerts a pull on all objects. Gravity can be seen in action every day. It is what makes an object fall to the ground when it is dropped. It is what keeps people and animals from floating off into space. It is what keeps the moon in its orbit around the Earth and the planets in their orbits around the sun. The pull of gravity is greater for objects that have greater mass. It is also greater on objects that are close together. For example, of the planets, Jupiter has the greatest gravitational pull on the Earth because it is so large. (The sun's enormous pull keeps Earth in its place, though!) However, Jupiter's pull is still only a tiny fraction of the moon's pull on the Earth because the moon is so much closer.

A skateboarder learns to overcome the force of gravity for some tricks, and to use it to his advantage for others. Gravity is what sends a skateboarder down the side of a half-pipe or bowl. It is also the force that he must overcome so that he can go up the other side and fly above the edge of the half-pipe or bowl. It is what causes him to return to the ground, and it is what causes him to fall off the board if he does not land just right.

Landing a skateboard successfully depends on the rider's ability to remain balanced over his center of gravity on the board. The center of gravity of an object is the average location of the mass of an object. Evenly shaped objects, such as a ball or a cube, have their mass distributed evenly, so their center of gravity is at or near their center. Objects that are top heavy fall over easily because they have more mass near the top than the bottom—a high center of gravity; gravity exerts more pull on the top part than on the bottom, so if they are tipped even slightly, they fall over. Objects with a lower center of gravity are more difficult to tip over because

Mass vs. Weight

The terms "mass" and "weight" are often used interchangeably, but scientifically speaking, they are not the same thing. Mass refers to how much matter is contained in an object. It is commonly used to describe how heavy something is, but mass is actually a property of inertia. That means it is an expression of the object's resistance to its motion being acted upon by an outside force (Newton's second law of motion). Think of a pound of feathers and a pound of lead. They each weigh the same—one pound, but the lead has more mass in it than the feathers and will require more force to move it. Mass also has little to do with size; a pillow is larger than a brick, but the brick has more mass.

Objects of greater mass tend to weigh more than objects of less mass, but weight is actually an expression of the force exerted on an object by gravity. The mass of an object is always the same, but its weight can change depending on where it is. For example, a bowling ball might weigh 16 pounds (7kg) on Earth because of the Earth's gravitational pull on it. If that bowling ball is moved to the moon, however, the ball will still have the same mass, but it will weigh only about 2.5 pounds (1.1kg) because the moon's gravitational pull is less than one-fifth of the Earth's. The same ball on the sun would weigh about 433 pounds (196kg) because of the sun's twenty-seven times greater gravitational pull.

Crouching down, a skateboarder lowers his center of gravity to help center his weight and reduce the chance of falling.

gravity pulls more on the lower part than on the upper. Most people, boys and men in particular, have their center of gravity just above the waist, because there is slightly more mass in the upper body than in the lower body. Skateboarders learn to maintain balance on their boards by bending their knees slightly and lowering their center of gravity, which helps center their weight evenly over the board and makes a fall less likely.

Friction

Friction, like gravity, is another physical force that a skateboarder needs but also must overcome in order to do anything on a skateboard. Friction is the resistance to movement encountered by an object sliding against a surface. The surface can be solid, like the ground; liquid, like water; or a gas, like air. The more irregular, or rough, a surface is, the more friction is created and the more the motion of the object is impeded. For example, a ball will roll much farther over glass than it will over grass. No surface is perfectly smooth, so any time one surface moves against another, there will be friction.

25342

Friction changes kinetic energy—the energy of motion—into heat energy. This can be seen when two sticks are rapidly rubbed together to start a fire, or when a person rubs his hands together vigorously to warm them on a cold day. Friction also changes kinetic energy into sound energy. The rougher the surfaces are, the louder the sound they make when they rub together. A skateboarder with worn-out wheels, riding on rough pavement, makes more noise than he would if he had new wheels riding on a smooth ramp. When friction changes kinetic energy into heat and sound, kinetic energy is lost. This is how friction causes a moving object such as a skateboard to slow down. Friction can

Isaac Newton

Isaac Newton was born on December 25, 1642, in Woolsthorpe, England, the son of a farmer who had died three months earlier. He was born prematurely and was not expected to live. When he was three, his mother remarried and went to live with her new husband, leaving him to be raised by his grandmother. They were reunited nine years later after her husband died. At school, Newton showed a talent for chemistry, and, in 1661, enrolled in Cambridge University, where he studied mathematics, physics, astronomy, and philosophy. In 1665 an epidemic of plague hit England, and Cambridge was closed temporarily. Back at home, he developed theories about calculus, optics, planetary motion, and gravity. In 1667 he returned to Cambridge as a professor and gained respect for his work on optics

and the nature of light. It was the height of the Scientific Revolution, and Newton worked alongside other famous scientists and philosophers such as Christiaan Huygens, Robert Hooke, Christopher Wren, Edmond Halley, and John Locke. In 1687 he published his most famous work, *Mathematical Principles of Natural Philosophy* (commonly called *Principia*), in which he described his three Laws of Motion and his discoveries about gravity and planetary motion. The work is considered one of the most influential scientific works in history and brought him international attention. Newton continued to earn awards and accolades, including two terms in the British Parliament. By his death in 1727, he was one of the most widely renowned scientists in the world. He was given a funeral fit for royalty and was buried in Westminster Abbey.

OFF THE HOOK

80.74 mph (129.94km/h)

The *Guinness World Records* fastest downhill speed on a skateboard—set by Mischo Erban in 2012.

also cause the surfaces involved to wear down over time, which anyone knows who has ever gotten a blister from digging a hole without using gloves! This is important to skateboarders who expect peak performance from their boards, because friction can wear down the surfaces of the wheels and their bearings.

There are several different kinds of friction, but three of them have the most effect on skateboarding. Rolling friction refers to the force that resists the movement of an object that is rolling across a surface. In skateboarding, rolling friction becomes a factor in two ways. First, friction is encountered by the ball bearings turning inside the wheel bearings. Clean, well-lubricated ball bearings turn much smoother and minimize the effects of friction inside the bearings. If the bearings are dirty, rusted, or corroded, there is more friction, so the wheels will not turn as smoothly, and the forward motion of the skateboard is slowed. Second, rolling friction has an effect on the way skateboard wheels move across a surface. Smooth wheels in good condition, without dings or flat spots, roll faster and smoother across whatever surface they are on. A mountainboarder relies on the rough tread of his tires to create friction with the ground and help him slow his descent down a steep hillside. The surface on which the rider is riding also matters. A smooth sidewalk gives a much faster ride than a gravel road, because of friction.

The second kind of friction that affects skateboarding is dry friction, also called sliding or kinetic friction. Dry friction resists the movement of two solid surfaces that are moving or sliding against each other. This is the kind of friction a skateboarder encounters when he grinds or slides his skateboard trucks along a surface such as a handrail or the edge of a step or bench. There are three laws of dry friction. First, the force of the friction is directly related to the load applied to the surface. In other words, the heavier the rider, the more dry friction he will encounter. The second

law states that the force of the friction is independent of the area of contact. This means that it does not matter whether the rider is grinding using both sets of trucks or just one. The force of friction is the same. The third law states that the force of friction is independent of the sliding velocity. This means that the friction is the same no matter how fast the rider is sliding over the surface.

The third kind of friction is static friction. Static friction is the friction between two objects at rest, relative to each other. Static friction is what keeps a wheel in contact with the ground and prevents it from slipping. Even though the wheel is moving, the part of it that is actually in contact with the ground is not moving relative to the ground. Without static friction, the wheels on the skateboard would just spin and would not move the skateboard forward.

Physics and Skateboard Tricks

Gravity and friction play a part in every kind of skateboarding activity. Even very simple tricks, however, demonstrate other concepts in physics that explain how the tricks are done. Tesler says:

> In a blur of flying acrobatics, skaters leap and skid over and onto obstacles, executing flips and turns of ever increasing complexity—all at top speeds. For onlookers and beginners, it can be hard to follow the action, let alone answer the question that springs naturally to mind: How on earth do they do that? While it may seem that modern skateboarders are defying the laws of physics, the truth is that they're just using them to their advantage.[11]

One of the simplest skateboard tricks is the hippie jump. The hippie jump demonstrates the concepts of velocity and projectile motion. Velocity is a physics term often used to mean speed, but they are not really the same thing. Speed is a measure of how far a moving object goes in a particular length of time, such as miles per hour. Velocity adds direction to distance and time. Velocity is called a vector quantity because of the addition of direction. The direction can be horizontal (side to side), vertical (up and down), or any other direction, but it must be in a straight line.

Projectile motion is a form of motion in which an object (called a projectile) is thrown into the air and moves along a curved path, like a rock being thrown, or a baseball being hit. The path followed by the projectile is called its trajectory. Projectile motion only occurs when there is one force applied at the beginning of the trajectory, such as the throw, after which, gravity and air friction act to bring the projectile back down.

For the hippie jump, the rider and the board are moving forward along the ground at a constant velocity. The rider then jumps into the air by bending his knees and pushing down on the board, propelling himself upward (Newton's Law of Force Pairs). By jumping, he becomes a projectile. He adds vertical direction but still also maintains his horizontal direction forward. When gravity takes over, he begins to go back down. While he is in the air, he travels along a curved trajectory called a parabolic arc. (Other examples of a parabolic arc include the path of water coming out of a drinking fountain, and the shape of the Gateway Arch in St. Louis, Missouri.) Because both rider and board continue to move forward with the same velocity, the board remains directly under the rider, and he lands safely back on the board.

The ollie is one of the first tricks a skateboarder learns because it is basic to almost all other tricks. It is similar to the hippie jump except that, for the ollie, both the rider and the board leave the ground. To make the board leave the

Velocity, momentum, and gravity play important roles in gaining enough speed to climb a bowl and perform an aerial trick.

ground, the rider begins his jump. As he jumps upward, he raises his arms up, giving himself more upward energy. At the same time, he pushes down very hard with his back foot on the rear kicktail of the board, causing it to strike the ground. The downward force of the rear of the board sends the front of the board upward like the nose of a rising airplane. A fraction of a second later, the force of the rear of the board striking the ground causes it to rebound, sending it upward as well (again, Newton's Law of Force Pairs). As the rider and the board move upward, the rider drags his front foot along the front kicktail, using friction between his foot and the grip tape to control the board and to pull it up even higher. At the top of the jump, he presses down with his front foot, which brings the back end of the board up to meet his back foot. At this point, it looks as if he is standing on the board in midair. Then gravity takes over, and the board and the rider return to the ground.

The frontside 180 adds another layer of complexity to the ollie by adding a 180-degree horizontal turn in the air so that when the rider lands, he is facing the opposite direction from where he started. It can be done on a flat surface, or in the air above the rim of a ramp. Making the board turn around in the air involves a physics concept called Conservation of Angular Momentum.

Conservation of Angular Momentum

Momentum is a measure of how much force it takes to get an object of a particular mass, going at a particular velocity, to stop. Linear momentum refers to momentum in a straight line. For example, if a runner loses his balance, he will fall down, but he will also continue to move forward as he falls because of momentum. The momentum of a moving object is a function of its mass and its velocity, and can be expressed by the simple mathematical equation $p = mv$, or momentum (represented by the letter p) equals mass (m) times velocity (v). A heavier or faster runner who falls has more forward momentum than a lighter or slower runner. He will fall farther forward, and will require more force to stop his fall.

Demonstrating Angular Momentum

The Law of Conservation of Angular Momentum can be difficult to understand, but you can demonstrate it for yourself very easily. Sit in a swiveling office chair, with your legs extended and your feet off the ground. Hold your arms straight out in front of you with palms together. Now start to swing your arms from side to side. Look at your feet. You will notice that as you swing your arms to the right, the chair turns slightly to the left. As you swing your arms around to the left, the chair turns to the right. As long as your arm swings are equally forceful in both directions, the chair will turn equally as well—angular momentum is conserved. However, if your arm swings are more forceful in one direction than the other, you will soon notice the chair gradually turning you in the direction opposite from the more forceful arm swing. This is because you are creating unbalanced momentum, or torque, in one direction, causing the chair to make up for it by turning more in the other direction. In this way, angular momentum is again conserved.

Angular momentum, on the other hand, is not linear— it is rotational. That means it is the amount of momentum an object has as it turns around an axis. (Imagine a Frisbee spinning through the air or the Earth rotating on its axis.) The Law of Conservation of Angular Momentum is somewhat similar to Newton's Law of Inertia. It says that angular momentum stays the same (with a measured value of zero) as long as there is no twisting force, or torque, acting on it in a direction opposite to its rotation. Conversely, if an object is not rotating, it cannot rotate unless torque causes it to rotate. When a skateboarder doing a frontside 180 is in midair, the only force acting on him is gravity, which does not exert torque. The skateboarder has to create the torque himself. He does this by rotating his upper and lower body in opposite directions. With his knees drawn up, and his arms extended out, he twists his lower body around. At the same time, his upper body rotates in the opposite direction. The rotations cancel out, or balance, each other, and angular momentum is conserved, or kept at zero. As soon as he lands, he can use force of the ground against the board to again create torque and turn his upper body around in line with his lower body.

Velocity, momentum, and gravity are also important for a skateboarder who wants to rise high enough above the edge of a half-pipe and perform complex maneuvers in midair. The faster the rider is going as he rides up the side of the pipe, the greater his momentum, the higher into the air he will go, and the more time he has to perform his aerial trick. Another force, however, called centripetal force, also factors in here. The skateboarder, in order to overcome this force, generates extra speed by doing a move called pumping.

Centripetal Force and Pumping

Centripetal force was described by Newton in 1684. It acts on an object that is moving along a circular path and keeps the object moving at a uniform speed along its circular path by drawing the object inward, toward the center of the circular path. Centripetal force is not actually a particular kind of force, like gravity or friction; other forces can act as a centripetal force. For example, gravity is the centripetal force that keeps a satellite in its orbit around the Earth and prevents it from flying into space. A tether ball spinning around a pole on the end of a rope is held in its circular path by the tension in the rope. If the rope breaks, the ball will go flying off in a straight line. A car that speeds around a sharp bend in the road is kept from veering off the road by centripetal force provided by the friction of its tires against the road.

A half-pipe is a curved path, which can be seen as part of a circle. When a skateboarder is moving up the side of the pipe, centripetal force comes from the friction force of the pipe surface against the skateboard, and tends to push him

toward the center of the circle. The friction also limits the rider's speed. In order to overcome the effects of friction, the rider needs to increase his speed up the side of the pipe. He does this by pumping. It is the same action that a child uses to gain height on a swing. "What you're doing is you're turning your body into a type of physical instrument that allows you to put energy back into the ride,"[12] says physicist and lifelong skater James Riordon. To pump, the rider crouches down on the board on the way down the side. At the bottom of the pipe, the rider straightens his legs and raises his arms in the air. Centripetal force makes it harder to do this on a curved path than on a straight one, so the extra energy needed to overcome the centripetal force actually adds energy to the entire moving system. The added energy helps increase his speed up the other side of the pipe, which gives him more height at the top.

Centripetal force allows Yojany Perez to climb a wall at a skateboarding event at the Ciudad Deportiva sporting complex in Havana, Cuba.

Of course, most skateboarders are not consciously aware of the principles of physics while they are doing an ollie, a frontside 180, or any other trick. Skateboarders learn by doing, by constant practice and perseverance. It is more about getting the "feel" of a trick than understanding the science behind it.

Skateboarder and writer Nan Adie says:

This *feel* for things takes experience to develop. You need to know your abilities and what is needed for the different types of tricks. Each trick you learn will be different. Every time you start a trick you will combine skateboarding physics to learn the technique to land it. Skaters are all over skateboarding physics, without even knowing it.[13]

CHAPTER **4**

Training and Conditioning for Skateboarding

T he average skateboarder may seem confused when asked about training for the sport. Most recreational skateboarders are young, healthy teens or young adults. They ride because it is fun and challenging and because it connects them with a peer group that shares their enthusiasm and general outlook on life. Most will say they never actually train specifically for skateboarding but that just doing it day after day provides all the physical training and skill development they need.

Skateboarding is certainly an excellent form of exercise by itself. Professional boarders, however, and those who wish to become professionals someday, understand the importance of maintaining the peak physical condition and sharp mastery of skills necessary to reach their goal. They devote a significant portion of their time to serious physical training and skills practice, no matter the season, the weather, or what other interesting things may be going on. Just as with other sports, success at this elite level requires dedication, focus, and sacrifice. Training for skateboarding, as for most other sports, involves developing several basic abilities, called biomotor abilities. Biomotor abilities—especially important for skateboarders—include strength, flexibility, balance, and endurance. Physical health is also maintained at its peak with proper nutrition and hydration, and by avoiding toxic substances such as cigarettes, drugs, and alcohol.

Muscles and Strength

Muscle strength is the ability of a muscle to exert force. Muscle strength is extremely important for the skateboarder. Strength helps the skateboarder maintain his center of gravity and improves stability on the board. It gives him the extra power he needs to increase his speed, especially for vert skating. It also allows him to maintain a high level of performance for a longer period of time without tiring. Strength training for skateboarding does not involve building large muscles. Rather, it is about developing strong muscles. Big muscles are not necessarily strong muscles, and in skateboarding, strength is more important than size.

Strength training helps skateboarders build strong—but not necessarily big—muscles.

The human body contains three different kinds of muscle tissue. Cardiac muscle is the muscle of the heart, and is found nowhere else in the body. It contracts, or shortens, during each heartbeat, sending blood out into the blood vessels. Smooth muscle is part of the lining of several hollow organs, such as the esophagus (food tube), stomach, urinary

bladder, and intestines. Smooth muscle contractions move substances such as food, urine, and feces through the organs. Skeletal muscle is the muscle responsible for movement. Every movement a person makes, from walking, running, and jumping to blinking, frowning, and wiggling the ears, is made possible by skeletal muscle. Examples of skeletal muscles include the biceps and triceps, located on the front and back of the upper arm; the quadriceps and hamstrings on the front and back of the thigh; and the rectus abdominus on the abdomen. There are approximately 640 named skeletal muscles in the human body. These are the muscles involved in strength training.

How Skeletal Muscles Work

Skeletal muscles are very complex structures. A skeletal muscle is made up of thousands of muscle cells, or fibers, which run the length of the muscle. Groups of muscle fibers work along with a nerve called a motor neuron, which transmits messages from the brain to the muscle and cause it to contract, or shorten. The muscle fibers, along with their motor neuron, are called a motor unit.

There are two basic kinds of muscle fibers: slow-twitch and fast-twitch. Slow-twitch fibers contract slowly and do not grow as large as fast-twitch, but tire less quickly than fast-twitch fibers. They are used for movements that require less strength but more endurance. Fast-twitch fibers contract more quickly and can grow larger, but they also tire sooner. Depending on their genetics, some people's muscles have more slow-twitch fibers; other people's contain more fast-twitch fibers. Athletes tend to do better at sports that favor their predominant type of muscle fiber. "There is great variability in the percentage of fiber types among athletes," says exercise physiologist Jason Karp. "For example, it is well known that endurance athletes have a greater proportion of slow-twitch fibers, while sprinters and jumpers have more fast-twitch fibers."[14] Skateboarding requires shorter, stronger bursts of energy, rather than long periods of endurance, so people with more fast-twitch fibers in their muscles tend to be more successful at it.

Skeletal muscles are attached to bones, usually at a joint, by tough, fibrous bands called tendons. Tendons are easy to see on the back of the hands and fingers and at the back of the heel (the Achilles tendon). When a skeletal muscle contracts, it pulls on the tendon attached to the bone at the joint and causes the bone to move. For example, when a person wants to bend his elbow, his brain sends a message to the motor units in the bicep, which contracts and pulls on the tendon at the elbow. This contraction pulls the lower arm up. To straighten the arm, the bicep relaxes and the triceps, on the back of the arm, contracts, pulling the lower arm back down.

Strength Training for Skateboarding

When the bicep contracts to raise the lower arm, it does not have to work very hard to do it because the lower arm does not weigh very much. However, if a person holds a heavy weight in his hand, the bicep must work much harder to overcome the greater force of gravity pulling on the object of greater mass (Isaac Newton's Second Law of Motion).

When a muscle is forced to work repeatedly against greater resistance, such as during weight training sessions, small microscopic tears occur in the muscle fibers. Over time, this kind of damage actually leads to increases in size and strength of the muscle. Fitness expert Gabe Mirkin explains:

> Nobody really knows how these hard bouts make muscles stronger, but the most likely theory depends on the fact that hard exercise damages muscle fibers. . . . The damaged muscle cells release tissue growth factors to heal the damaged muscle fibers, and if the athlete allows muscle soreness to disappear before exercising again, muscle fibers become larger and increase in number by splitting to form new fibers.[15]

A strength training workout for skateboarding, as for any sport, begins with a careful warm-up for the muscles, including gentle stretching. Warm-up activities can include walking on a treadmill or elliptical trainer, running in place, or jumping rope. The warm-up prepares the muscles for hard work by increasing blood flow to the muscle tissue, raising the temperature of the muscles, relaxing them, and by increasing flexibility in the joints. Muscles and joints that have not been properly warmed up before strenuous exercise are more prone to injury.

The actual strength training part of the workout focuses on working the muscle groups most important for skateboarding. Skateboarding requires strength mainly in the muscles of the legs and core (abdomen, upper, and lower back). A rider spends a lot of time in a crouch position on the board, and strong legs are needed to support and maintain that position. The legs guide the direction of the board, provide the force needed to do tricks, and absorb the shock of landing aerial tricks. Strength training exercises for the legs include calf raises, leg presses, squats, leg extensions, and deadlifts. Strong core muscles are essential for maintaining balance and for doing flips and turns. There are many exercises that build strength in the core, such as crunches, Russian twists, leg lifts, planks, and rowing.

OFF THE HOOK

75%

Proportion of skeletal muscle made up of water.

Stretching

Doing gentle stretches after the pre-workout warm-up helps improve performance during the workout by improving flexibility of the muscles, tendons, and joints. After a strength workout, gentle muscle stretching improves flexibility further and helps minimize soreness and tightness in the muscles. Flexibility is the ability of a joint to move through a wide range of motion. How flexible a joint is depends on the tendons and muscles that move it, as well as the tough bands called ligaments that hold bones together at the joint. Flexibility is important to the skateboarder because flexible muscles and joints move more easily and can move through a greater range of motion. This lets the rider do more complex tricks and helps him avoid injury during uncontrolled falls. "Stretching is an essential part of physical fitness," says health educator Raginee Edwards. "Routine stretching may slow the degeneration of joints, reduce the risk of injury, improve posture, enhance muscular relaxation, reduce or manage stress, improve functional performance, and promote circulation."[16]

There are two kinds of stretches: static and ballistic. Static stretches are done by slowly moving the muscle into the stretched position, holding it there for twenty to thirty

Stretching before a competition helps muscles and joints move more easily and through a greater range of motion.

seconds, and then releasing the stretch. An example is a calf stretch or a hamstring stretch. They can be done by the person himself (active stretching) or they can be done by a machine or another person who moves the body part into the stretch position and then holds it there (passive stretching).

Ballistic stretches include a series of bounces during the stretch that move the joint past its normal range. Ballistic stretching, however, can be hazardous. Edwards explains:

Ballistic stretching is no longer considered a safe way of stretching and may even cause injury, due to the quick forceful movement beyond your range of motion. A safer modification of this stretch is called dynamic stretching, in which you use movement and/or speed to gradually increase range of motion. It is done in a controlled fashion, however, as opposed to bouncing your body forcefully beyond its range of motion. [Arm circles, or windmills, are an example of a dynamic stretch.] If you are choosing between ballistic and static stretching, then static stretching is the winner. It's a gentle and effective way to stretch when performed properly.[17]

Any strength training program should always be done with proper instruction in form and technique. Improper form decreases results and can cause injury.

It is very important for the athlete to allow the muscles time to rest and recover between intense workouts so that the healing and strengthening process can take place. If he does not, the muscles can remain damaged and actually become weaker. Low-intensity workouts, however, can be done while the muscles are healing, without long-term damage.

"If the athlete exercises at low intensity during recovery," says Mirkin, "his muscles will become more fibrous and resistant to injury when he stresses his muscles with the next intense bout of exercise."[18]

Balance

In biomechanics, balance is the ability of an object to maintain a vertical line of gravity (its center of mass) over a base of support with minimal sway. In people, balance is a very complex skill. Balance allows us to see clearly while moving our head, so that we do not get dizzy. It allows us to tell which way is up. It lets us determine how fast and in which direction an object is moving, and it helps us to automatically make adjustments so that we can remain stable in varying conditions, such as stepping onto a trampoline from solid ground or stepping off a moving escalator.

In skateboarding, balance is the ability of the rider to maintain his center of gravity over the board without swaying so much that he falls off. A good sense of balance is critical for skateboarding. Balance keeps a rider on his board, helps him to maintain control of the board, and allows him to maneuver the board through moves and tricks. Strong legs and a strong core are necessary for maintaining that line of gravity, so strength training helps improve balance. Balance also involves input from three other sensory systems: the visual system, the somatosensory system, and the vestibular system. The input from these three systems is coordinated by the brain to achieve balance.

The visual system provides information to the brain from the eyes. It lets a person identify and recognize objects based on information stored in his memory. It tells a person how large things are or how far away they are. It tells him how he must move his body in relation to other objects. The skateboarder's visual system helps him maintain balance by telling him how fast he is going and how far away obstacles are so that he can prepare to meet them.

The somatosensory system sends a lot of various information to the brain from the skin, muscles, and joints. It tells a person if he is moving or standing still, if he is standing straight up or leaning over, which way his head is turned, and the nature of the surface he is walking on—ice, gravel, or grass, for example. The somatosensory system tells the skateboarder when he is in the air and when he is on the ground, if he is leaning right or left, or if he has hit an obstacle on the ground.

The vestibular system is located in the inner ear. It provides information to the brain about motion, spatial orientation, and equilibrium. Structures in the vestibular system

WORKING TOGETHER FOR BALANCE

Vestibular system: The primary sensory system that regulates balance and contributes to the body's sense of direction is in the inner ear. Fluid inside special organs moves thousands of microscopic hairs that send signals about the direction of the body's movement to the brain.

Visual system: The eyes and their pathways of information to the brain tells the body where it is in relation to other objects.

Somatosensory system: Receptors in the skin, skeletal muscles, joints, bones, and internal organs send the brain information on pressure, vibration, temperature, and other factors used by the body to decide how to move.

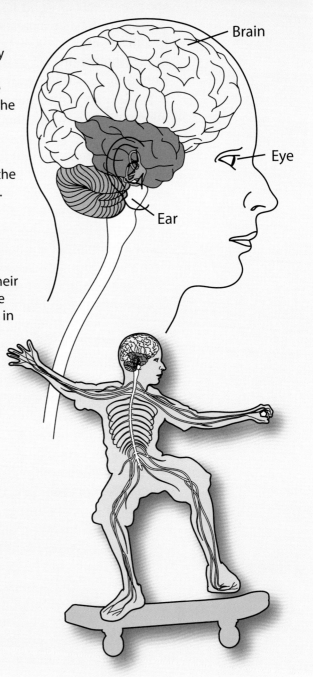

tell us if an object is moving in a straight line (linear movement) or spinning in a circle (rotational movement). Spatial orientation tells us how objects are arranged in space. For example, it lets us know if something is right side up or upside down. Equilibrium means that all the input from our five senses makes sense. For example, if a person is sitting in a car and the car next to him backs up, the visual information may make him think for a moment that his car is actually moving forward, even though somatosensory information tells him that he is still. This conflicting information causes a temporary loss of equilibrium until the vestibular system overrides the conflicting information.

As long as there are no problems with these three systems, all this sensory information is coordinated in the brain, and balance is maintained. Balance is learned at a young age and is improved through practice and repetition of movement. The more a person practices, the easier it is for the body to learn to balance. For example, gymnasts must practice for many years in order to perform well on the balance beam. Skateboarding takes constant practice in order to learn how to balance on a moving skateboard and do tricks without falling. Skateboarders can practice balance simply by standing on their board or other unstable surfaces, and feeling how their body adjusts to every slight movement. Standing with the feet close together or with the eyes closed, standing on one leg, on the heels or on the toes, and standing on narrower surfaces such as rails, adds difficulty and improves balance faster.

Balance trainers of several kinds are also available for skateboarders to sharpen their balance skills. Some balance trainers look like skateboard decks with a roller under them. They let the rider stand on the board and practice maintaining balance on the roller. Other balance trainers consist of an inflatable disc that can be made firmer or softer. Some of these, such as a Bosu, have a rigid standing surface on one side.

Endurance

Skateboards are not propelled by motors or wind or water but by human muscle power alone, so skateboarders, whether participating in a weekend competition or just transporting themselves across town, need to build up a moderate level of endurance. Endurance, also called stamina or cardio fitness, is the ability to perform work over a period of time without fatiguing. An athlete with good endurance can perform for a long time without tiring and can continue to perform well even after he has become tired.

Like all cells in the human body, when a muscle cell is working, a series of complex chemical reactions takes place inside the cell. The process by which a cell carries out these reactions is called metabolism. Metabolism works very much like the way a car engine runs. In most cells (including muscles), glucose, a form of sugar, is the fuel for metabolism. Oxygen is also necessary, in order for the cell to use the glucose as fuel. Just as a car produces waste products in the form of exhaust, the cell also produces waste products of metabolism. The waste products of metabolism are carbon dioxide (CO_2) and water, which are removed by the body through the lungs. As a person increases the intensity of exercise, his cell metabolism speeds up and waste products are produced. His heartbeat and breathing become harder and faster in order to supply the muscles with the oxygen they need to drive metabolism and remove metabolic waste products from the body.

For these reasons, endurance depends on excellent cardio-respiratory fitness. This means having healthy lungs to draw in air, extract the oxygen from it, and get the oxygen into the bloodstream. The lungs also have to be able to filter the CO_2 and water out of the blood and expel them through breathing. It means having a strong heart to pump the blood to and from the lungs and healthy blood vessels to carry the blood to and from all the cells of the

Skateboarders, such as these racers on the Pikes Peak course outside Colorado Springs, Colorado, need a high level of endurance.

Interval Training and Teens

Interval training involves doing short bursts of high-intensity exercise, alternating with periods of rest between the intervals. A 2011 study published in the *American Journal of Human Biology* compared high-intensity interval training with more traditional continuous endurance training to see how each kind of exercise affected common indicators of heart health in teenagers. In the study, fifty-seven teens (forty-seven boys, ten girls) from ages fifteen to seventeen were divided into three groups. One group did high-intensity interval training (HIT), one did moderate-intensity continuous training (MOD), and the third group did no training at all (the control group). The teens in the exercise groups did three workouts a week for seven weeks. The MOD group exercised for a total of 420 minutes; the HIT group exercised for a total of only 63 minutes. At the end of the seven weeks, the teens were measured for several indicators of heart health. Both the HIT and MOD groups showed significant improvement in weight, blood pressure, body fat percentage, and other indicators of cardiac health. The conclusion was that short, high-intensity workouts are just as effective as longer, moderate workouts, but are more time-efficient.

body. Cardio-respiratory fitness is maximized through endurance training.

Training for Endurance

Training for endurance means doing exercises and activities that work the heart and lungs beyond their normal resting state. Endurance training can be continuous or at intervals. Continuous training means doing the activity at a steady pace and intensity for forty-five to ninety minutes. Interval training alternates short, high-intensity bursts of activity with low-intensity recovery periods. Of the two, interval training is thought to be more effective for increasing the efficiency of the heart and lungs and increasing endurance. Common endurance training activities include bicycling, running, and swimming.

Endurance training provides a variety of physical improvements that benefit the skateboarder's overall health as well as his skating performance. In the lungs, endurance training increases blood flow and improves the exchange of oxygen and CO_2. It strengthens the heart so that it can pump more blood with each beat (its cardiac output). It increases the volume of blood in the body and the number of red blood cells, which are the blood cells that carry oxygen. In the muscles, endurance training improves blood flow to the muscle cells and speeds healing and muscle growth.

Training and Nutrition

No amount of training can be effective without proper nutrition. Without the right kinds of fuel, the human machine cannot perform at its best. Skateboarders need strength and endurance in order to excel at their sport, and proper care of the body is essential to achieving this goal. For skateboarders—as with any active person—the right balance of nutrients provides the strength, endurance, and energy needed to enjoy the sport to the fullest.

Nutrients are the chemicals in food that provide the cells with the fuel necessary for them to perform their functions. Nutrients provide energy in the form of calories. Calories are actually a measure of energy. They are necessary even during sleep, because energy is needed by all cells at all times. The more active a person is, the more calories he needs to take in to provide the energy he needs. It is important, however, to take in the needed calories in the form of healthy foods that provide a good balance of nutrients. The major nutrients important for optimal health are carbohydrates, fats, and protein. While not classified as a nutrient, water is also necessary for health.

Carbohydrates

Carbohydrates, commonly referred to as carbs, are of two types: simple and complex. Simple carbohydrates are simple sugar molecules such as glucose, fructose, and lactose. They are digested quickly and provide short bursts of energy. Simple carbs are found in foods such as white sugar, soft drinks, pastries, dairy products, fruit, pasta, white bread, and white rice. Simple carbs should be eaten only in small amounts. Complex carbohydrates are larger chains of three or more sugar molecules. They take longer to digest in the body but provide longer-lasting energy. They are found in foods such as whole grain breads, oatmeal, brown rice, beans, and vegetables.

Carbs are important for skateboarders because they are the body's preferred source of energy. One gram (about one-third of an ounce) of complex carbs provides four calories of energy. When a person eats carbs, the liver breaks them down into a simple sugar called glucose, which is used as fuel by many cells, especially brain cells. Extra glucose is stored in the liver and the muscles in a form called glycogen. If the body needs extra fuel for any reason, it converts the stored glycogen back into glucose.

Fats

If a person exercises for a long time, or if he is injured or very ill, he may use up his available stores of carbohydrates for energy or healing. If that happens, the body turns next to fats as fuel. When fats are digested, they are broken down into glycerol and fatty acids. The glycerol can be converted to glucose by the liver and used for calories. One gram of fat provides nine calories of energy. Excess calories in the body are stored in fatty tissue called adipose tissue. Visceral adipose tissue is located within the abdomen, around the internal organs. Subcutaneous adipose tissue is located under the skin.

Fats may be solid or liquid. They are found in both plant and animal sources such as dairy products, meats, fish, egg yolks, lard, oils, and nuts. Fats perform several important functions in the human body and are an important part of the diet. Fats provide necessary chemicals called essential fatty acids (EFAs), which the body does not make and which must be obtained from food. They are necessary for proper

Sugar and the Brain

The brain never sleeps. It is always active, even when the remainder of the body is at rest. Brain cells (neurons) require twice as much energy to function as other cells, and half of those fuel requirements are spent communicating signals to the rest of the body. Glucose is the fuel of choice for the brain. An inadequate amount of glucose in the brain has been shown to decrease the ability to learn and remember.

If too much glucose is taken in all at once, however, it can actually be harmful to the brain. When a person takes in a large amount of glucose, for example, by drinking a large non-diet soda or eating a big piece of cake, the pancreas is stimulated to release a hormone called insulin. Insulin tells cells throughout the body to take the glucose out of the blood and store it for later use. Neurons, however, cannot store glucose. They need a constant supply of it delivered by the bloodstream. If the supply of glucose is removed from the blood by other cells in response to insulin, then there is not enough left for the neurons, and their function suffers. The person may feel weak, confused, nervous, and unable to think clearly or pay attention. This is called hypoglycemia (low blood sugar), and it can impair a person's ability to carry out his activities, including skateboarding.

eyesight and brain development in babies and children. They provide protection and insulation for the internal organs to help keep them warm. It is also used to help utilize other nutrients such as certain vitamins and minerals.

Contrary to popular belief, fats are not as much of a factor in obesity and heart disease as was once thought. Dietary fats are classified as either saturated or unsaturated. Unsaturated fat is considered healthier fat and should provide most of a person's fat intake. They are found in nuts and seeds, seed and vegetable oils, and seafood. Saturated fats are considered unhealthy because excessive amounts can lead to clogged arteries and heart disease later in life. They are found in fatty meats, full-fat dairy products, and some plant sources such as coconut oil, palm oil, and cocoa butter. They are also used in many packaged foods such as chips, cookies, and crackers. Saturated fats should be consumed in limited amounts. Trans fats are artificial, manmade fats used in some margarines, fast food, and in many processed foods. They are usually listed on food labels as "partially hydrogenated" fat. They also contribute to clogged arteries and may contribute to some kinds of cancer. Trans fats should be avoided altogether.

Protein

Many people tend to think of protein only as the building blocks of muscle. While that is true, proteins are so much more. Protein molecules are located in every organ and in every cell of the body. Hair, fingernails, and the lens of the eye are all made of pure protein. Enzymes that digest foods, such as lactase and pepsin, are proteins. Some hormones, such as insulin, needed for sugar metabolism, are protein molecules. Disease-fighting antibodies are proteins. The protein molecule hemoglobin is called a transport protein. It binds to oxygen in the blood and carries it to all the cells. Even the genetic molecule DNA is actually a protein.

When a protein is digested, it is broken down into smaller components called amino acids. These are the real building blocks. Amino acids are then built back into other protein molecules and used for their hundreds of uses, such as tissue repair and muscle building. Proteins are found in animal products such as red meat, fish, eggs, poultry, and cheeses. They can also be found in vegetable sources such as grains, nuts, and legumes. Animal proteins are called complete proteins because they contain all nine of the amino acids humans must get from their diet. Plant proteins are incomplete, but they can be completed by eating combinations of plant sources, such as whole grain bread, with peanut butter or brown rice with beans.

One gram of protein produces about four calories of energy. Because of protein's critical role in cell and organ function, however, it is not used by the body as a calorie source as long as there are adequate carb and fat stores available. Protein is only used as a last resort, when there is no other

Maintaining Skills in Winter

Skateboarding is mostly done outside, during warmer months. In areas where winters are cold and snowy, there are ways to still be able to ride and to keep skills sharp.

Flatground tricks, such as ollies, can be practiced inside a garage, and an indoor skate park is an obvious alternative, if there is one nearby. Skate parks may charge a fee, but it is usually not very much, and memberships are often available.

Indoor training equipment and practice tools, such as balance trainers and ollieblocks (a tool for practicing ollies without rolling), are a good way to maintain and sharpen skills over the winter.

Watching skateboard videos is a way to learn about how professionals perform their tricks and techniques.

If the ground is covered in snow, snowskates and snowdecks are a possibility. Snowskates are like a cross between a skateboard and a snowboard. Snowdecks, also called bi-level snowskates, look like skateboard decks with trucks attached to a small ski on the bottom.

The winter is also a good time to spend training—increasing strength, balance, and endurance by working out at a gym or at home, for instance.

If all else fails, playing skateboard video games can help maintain enthusiasm for riding until the weather gets better—even if they don't help improve skills or physical fitness!

choice for survival, such as during starvation. The use of protein as fuel causes a person to waste away, a condition called cachexia (ka-KEX-ia). Prolonged cachexia eventually leads to death.

Staying Hydrated

Water is necessary for all life on Earth. In the human body, water serves many purposes. It is an essential part of cell metabolism, as well as a byproduct of it. Water allows

Skateboarding causes a great deal of water loss through breathing and sweating.

chemicals to move in and out of cells and keeps them balanced. It is the major component of blood and supports blood pressure. It makes up 80 percent of the total weight of the brain. It regulates body temperature and lubricates joints. It carries waste products out of the body through the kidneys and digestive tract.

Because skateboarding is done mostly outside, during warmer months, a great deal of water is lost through breathing and sweating. Sweating also causes loss of important chemicals called electrolytes, which make sweat taste salty. It is very important to stay adequately hydrated during any physical activity, but especially in the heat. Inadequate water intake leads to a condition called dehydration. Dehydration interferes with both physical and mental performance. Severe dehydration on a hot day can cause body temperature to rise to dangerous levels, a condition called heat stroke. Skateboarders should keep a supply of fluids such as sports drinks available, which help replace water, carbohydrates, and electrolytes.

Skateboarding Injuries

Training and conditioning the body goes a long way toward preventing injuries in skateboarding, but because of the nature of the sport, injuries are almost unavoidable. As skateboarding has become more popular, and as kids start skating at younger ages, skateboarding injuries have become more common. According to the American Academy of Orthopedic Surgeons: "In 2011, skateboard-related injuries accounted for more than 78,000 emergency room visits among children and adolescents (nineteen years old or younger). On average, about 52 percent of skateboard injuries involve children under age fifteen. Most of the children injured are boys (average 85 percent)."[19]

Most skateboarding injuries are to the face, arms, head, and legs. Most of them happen because of lack of experience, lack of physical strength, attempting tricks beyond one's skill level, and not using protective equipment such as helmets and pads. More than half of them are caused by falls when the skateboard hits an irregular surface such as a rock or hole in the pavement. Falls also occur when a rider attempts a trick that he has not mastered yet, such as grinding down a stair railing, and loses control of the board. Falls can also result from speed wobble and wheel bite. Speed wobble happens when the rider is going very fast on the skateboard, especially downhill, and the vibrations from the surface cause the trucks to begin turning rapidly from side to side on their own. The board starts wobbling uncontrollably and the rider is thrown off. Wheel bite occurs when the trucks are too loose or the wheels are too big, and the wheels come into contact with the bottom of the board, especially during a turn. The friction of the wheels against the board can cause the board to stop suddenly and the rider is thrown off. Many of the most serious injuries happen when a skateboarder is hit by a vehicle while riding in the street, especially after dark.

Types of Skateboarding Injuries

Skateboarding injuries range from minor, requiring little or no treatment, to very severe or even fatal. The most minor skateboarding injuries include abrasions (scrapes), lacerations (cuts), and contusions (bruises). Abrasions happen when a skateboarder's skin is dragged along the ground during a fall. This type of injury bleeds a little, and stings, but is easily treated at home with thorough cleansing, antibiotic ointment, and a sterile bandage.

Lacerations are cuts that go deeper through the skin than abrasions. They tend to bleed more, especially if they are large. The first goal in treating a laceration is to control bleeding by putting pressure on the cut with a cloth. If the bleeding stops quickly, the cut can be treated like an abrasion. If the bleeding does not stop, or if the cut is very deep, it may need medical attention, including stitches.

Contusions happen when a body part impacts a surface, but the skin is not damaged. Small blood vessels under the surface break and bleeding into the soft tissues under the skin or in the muscle occurs. This is what

The most common skateboarding injuries include lacerations, which should be treated by putting pressure on the cut with a cloth until the bleeding stops.

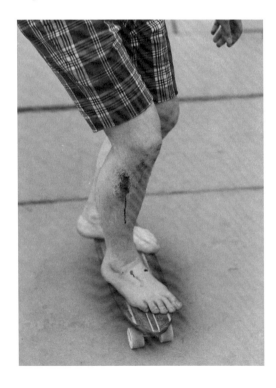

causes the bluish-purple color of a bruise. Contusions are usually minor, and can be treated at home with over-the-counter pain medication and ice to control swelling.

Contusions can also be serious, however, if there is a lot of swelling deep in the muscle. Many skeletal muscles, such as those in the arms and legs, are surrounded by a tough, whitish sheath called a capsule, which restricts the amount of space in which the muscle can swell. If the muscle swells a lot and stays swollen, the blood vessels that supply it can become compressed, which restricts the muscle's blood supply. This sets up a serious condition called compartment syndrome. Compartment syndrome is very painful. It can cause death of the muscle tissue and requires surgery, with a long recovery time, in order to correct it.

Sprains and Strains

Sprains and strains are very common in skateboarding and usually happen during a fall. In December 2012, Mimi Knoop, professional boarder and women's vert X Games medalist, found that out firsthand: "I was skating the Vans Combi pool (which is 12 feet deep) and fell, in the corner, on my foot, she explains. "My foot folded inward on itself, and I thought I broke my ankle. It immediately swelled and bruised."[20] An MRI revealed that she had not broken the bone but had sustained a severe ankle sprain.

A sprain is an injury to a ligament. Ligaments are tough, fibrous bands that hold the bones together at a joint. They support the skeleton and prevent joints from moving in abnormal directions. For example, ligaments in the ankle function to prevent the foot from turning too far sideways, and in the knee to prevent the knee from bending forward. If a joint is suddenly moved in an abnormal way, such as during an accident or fall, the ligament can be overstretched or torn. This is a sprain, and it makes the joint unstable.

OFF THE HOOK

30%

Proportion of skateboard injuries sustained by those who have been skating for less than a week.

Symptoms include sudden sharp pain, swelling, and bruising of the skin. Skateboarders can get sprains by landing awkwardly during a fall. They most commonly occur to the knee, ankle, or wrist.

Sprains are classified as Grade I, II, or III, depending on the extent of the damage to the ligament. The main goal of the treatment of sprains is to minimize swelling and pain, and to allow the ligaments time to heal. Grades I and II can usually be treated with the RICE method: rest, ice, compression with a snug bandage, and elevation of the joint. Crutches may be necessary for a while to allow a knee or

Falling the Right Way

Falling is an unavoidable part of skateboarding, especially for young or inexperienced riders. The chances of being injured because of a fall can be minimized if the rider knows how to fall. The goal of falling correctly is to minimize the force of the impact on any one part of the body. If a rider realizes he is losing his balance, he should crouch down on the board so that he does not have as far to fall. Lowering the center of gravity in this way also may help him regain his balance and avoid the fall altogether. If the fall is unavoidable, however, the best way to land is on a fleshier part of the body rather than on a bony part. He should try to relax his muscles, rather than stiffen up. This lessens the force of the impact. He should also pull his arms close in to his body, try to land with as much body surface as possible, and roll with the fall, so that the force of the fall is more evenly distributed, rather than all on one part. This is not easy, since the natural instinct is to brace for a fall by extending the arms. That is why wrist injuries are so common.

Beginners should learn how to fall from experienced riders. There are also lots of Internet videos about the correct way to fall. Falling can be practiced with a mat, on grass, or on another soft surface.

ankle to rest. Grade III sprains may need surgery to fix them and can cause permanent instability of the joint. Physical therapy to improve strength and motion of the joint is also helpful following a sprain. Knoop's sprain was a Grade III. She did not have surgery, but her injury also included over-stretched nerves in her ankle. "To top it off," she says, "I also suffered nerve damage. I couldn't walk on uneven surfaces, like sand, for months. I also couldn't stretch without getting zapped [from the nerve damage]."[21]

A strain is similar to a sprain except that it affects a muscle or a tendon rather than a ligament. Strains are caused by overstretching or tearing the muscle or tendon. For skateboarders, strains commonly occur in the muscles of the lower back because they are involved in keeping balance and in doing twisting tricks such as the frontside 180. Strains in the muscles of the feet, thighs, neck, and groin area are also common. Like sprains, strains are classified as Grade I, II, or III. Grade I is sometimes called a pulled muscle. Grade II involves more tearing, but the muscle is still intact and can be used. A Grade III strain, however, involves complete rupture, or breakage, of the muscle, or a complete tearing of the muscle away from its tendons. In this case, the muscle cannot contract at all.

Symptoms of a muscle strain are sharp pain in the muscle and trouble using the affected body part. Grade III strains also include an obvious deformity in the shape of the muscle and considerable bleeding into the muscle tissue. Grade III strains may require surgery to repair the torn muscle. Lower grade strains can be treated with the RICE method, followed by a program of gentle stretches and strengthening exercises. Sprains and strains can be avoided by performing proper warm-up exercises and stretching before riding to keep the muscles and joints relaxed and flexible.

Knee Injuries

Knee injuries happen in skateboarding because of awkward landings during falls, or if the rider has to jump off his board suddenly and lands badly. Injuries occur when the knee is forcibly twisted or rotated, or if it is impacted from the side.

A DANGEROUS SPORT?

Skateboarding is inherently dangerous, and skateboarders should always follow all safety precautions. However, comparison of US data of injuries from a variety of sporting activities shows that skateboarding results in fewer injuries than many other, more popular sports.

Activity group and estimated number of injuries:

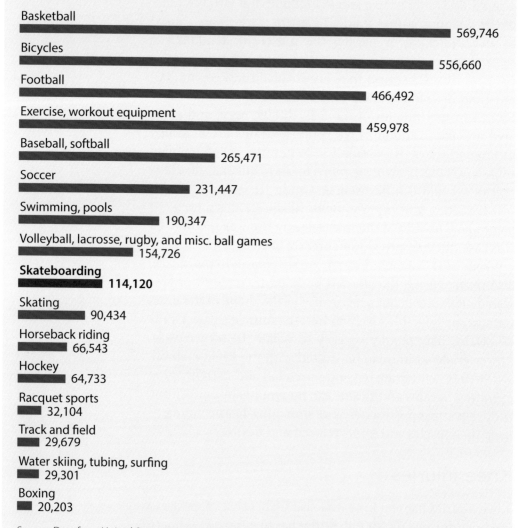

Basketball
569,746

Bicycles
556,660

Football
466,492

Exercise, workout equipment
459,978

Baseball, softball
265,471

Soccer
231,447

Swimming, pools
190,347

Volleyball, lacrosse, rugby, and misc. ball games
154,726

Skateboarding
114,120

Skating
90,434

Horseback riding
66,543

Hockey
64,733

Racquet sports
32,104

Track and field
29,679

Water skiing, tubing, surfing
29,301

Boxing
20,203

Source: Data from United States Consumer Product Safety Commission. "National Electronic Injury Surveillance System Data Highlights: 2012." www.cpsc.gov/en/Research--Statistics/NEISS-Injury-Data.

Most commonly, a knee injury involves a tear to the cartilage or ligaments in the knee joint.

Cartilage in the knee is called the meniscus. There are two of them: the medial meniscus near the inner side of the knee and the lateral meniscus near the outer side. These C-shaped pieces of cartilage act as a cushion and shock absorber between the femur (thigh bone) and the tibia (shin bone). A tear to a meniscus causes swelling and sharp pain in the knee, especially when the knee is straightened. There may be a clicking or popping sensation when the knee is bent. The knee may also lock and be difficult to bend. Minor meniscal tears can be treated with rest and physical therapy, including muscle-strengthening exercises. More severe tears, or tears that do not respond to nonsurgical treatment, may require surgery to remove or repair the torn part of the meniscus, followed by physical therapy.

There are four major ligaments in the knee that hold the femur and tibia in place and stabilize the knee joint. The most common ligament injury in the knee is to the anterior cruciate ligament, or ACL. Most ACL tears are caused by sudden changes in direction or by pivoting on the knee during a landing. When the ACL tears, there may be a popping sensation, and the knee gives out. There is significant pain and rapid swelling. The injury is confirmed with a magnetic resonance image, or MRI, a special kind of test that shows soft tissues inside the body that regular X-rays cannot show. Treatment for ACL tears depends on the severity of the tear and may include the RICE method, anti-inflammatory pain medications, physical therapy, or surgery to repair the ligament.

OFF THE HOOK

6 weeks

The average length of time needed for a broken wrist to heal in a healthy teenager.

Fractures

A fracture is a broken bone. Bones are rigid and strong, but with enough force, they can and do break. Fractures occur often in skateboarding because of uncontrolled falls or bad landings. The most common fracture for skateboarders happens in the small forearm bones near the wrist when riders attempt to break their fall by extending their arms forward. There are several kinds of fractures, depending on how the break happened. Some fractures are very minor. For example, a stress fracture is a small crack in the bone which happens after repeated stress caused by frequent impacts. They are very common in the lower legs and feet, especially in sports such as track, basketball, and skateboarding, which involve a lot of hard landing on the feet. Stress fractures can be too small to be seen on an X-ray, but they cause pain and swelling, and require rest and a cast or splint until they heal.

Another type of fracture is a stable fracture, in which the bone breaks straight across or at an angle, but the broken ends are still lined up with each other. If the ends are not in alignment, an orthopedic surgeon can manipulate the broken limb under anesthesia with an X-ray machine, until the ends are realigned. This is called a closed (no incision) reduction. Such fractures may need just a cast for them to

Uncontrolled falls or bad landings are the cause of most fractured bones in skateboarding.

How Bones Heal

Human bones have a remarkable ability to heal themselves, even without medical intervention. Three kinds of bone cells are responsible for bone growth and repair: osteoclasts, osteoblasts, and chondroblasts.

Osteoclasts break down old bone tissue so that it can be replaced with new bone by osteoblasts.

Chondroblasts form new cartilage tissue. After a fracture, bone healing begins almost immediately. It takes place in four stages. First, blood from the inside of the bone forms a clot, or hematoma, around the break called a fracture hematoma. This helps to stabilize the break. Tiny new blood vessels begin to grow almost immediately inside the hematoma. Then, after several days, collagen cells (the major protein in bone) and cartilage cells are formed and start to turn the hematoma into a stronger structure called a soft callus. As the callus toughens, it begins to bridge the gap between the broken ends of the bone. About three weeks later, osteoblasts move in and begin to form new bone cells; this turns the soft callus into a hard bone callus. During the final stage, called remodeling, blood supply improves. Osteoclasts and osteoblasts continue the work of removing dead bone cells and making new ones, restoring the bone to its original shape and strength.

heal. More complex fractures may need surgery to realign the bone fragments, along with metal plates and screws to hold them in place. This is called an open reduction with internal fixation, or ORIF. A compound fracture is one in which the bone is broken in more than one place. A fracture in which the bone is shattered in several small pieces is called a comminuted fracture. An open fracture is one in which the broken end of the bone has pierced the skin, or the impact has broken the skin at the point of the fracture. Open fractures are especially serious because there is a risk of infection in the bone.

Even professional skaters can fall badly enough to break a bone. In July 2010, skateboarding legend Tony Hawk fell during a routine vert trick at a demonstration performance in Anaheim, California. The fall broke his pelvis and caused internal bleeding. At the hospital, he tweeted: "I will no longer take walking for granted. Just took a 20-foot stroll around the room; it might as well have been 20 miles."[22]

In October 2013, fourteen-year-old Tom Schaar, the youngest ever X Games gold medalist, landed badly while attempting to skate Tony Hawk's loop ramp. Schaar was at the top of the loop when he fell to the ground and shattered his right shoulder. He was taken to the hospital and had surgery to fix the fracture.

Facial Injuries

In March 2011, a report was submitted to the California legislature about injuries to skateboarders in skate parks. The report stated: "A total of 792 injuries were reported between 2002 and 2010. Facial injuries were the most common, followed by injuries to the ankle, head, and arm."[23]

Injuries to the face happen to skateboarders when they fall forward and land on the face. The most common facial injuries include facial lacerations, broken or lost teeth, and fractures of the upper or lower jaw, nose, cheekbone, or eye socket. In August 2011, Hawk broke one of his front teeth in a fall during a skating demonstration in Jacksonville, Florida. That same week, hip-hop artist and avid boarder Lil' Wayne fell on his face while skating in St. Louis, Missouri, and needed nine stitches above his left eye. In July 2013, Brazilian skateboarder Bob Burnquist was trying to win his sixth gold medal at the X Games Big Air Competition when, from the top of the ramp, he took a nasty fall, landing on his face and breaking his nose. "I just snapped out too much [at the top of the ramp]," he said afterward. "I knew I was [landing] low, but I wanted to try to make it. But that was quite a punch."[24]

Treatment for facial injuries depends on the type and location of the injury. Minor cuts and scrapes can be treated with thorough cleansing, antibiotic ointment, and a sterile dressing. Broken teeth require a visit to a dentist for evaluation of the damage. Fractured facial bones may need surgery to repair them, depending on their severity and location. Any facial injury should be checked out by a doctor, however, because facial injuries can also indicate head or neck injuries that are not as obvious.

Head Injuries

On a spring day in 2009, Chad Crawford and his friend Jared Lloyd went skateboarding. As they sped down a long hill, both of them experienced speed wobble and lost control of their boards. They jumped off, but Crawford lost his balance, rolled a few times, and landed hard on the back of his head. He was not wearing a helmet.

"I guess people my age just find it childish to wear helmets," Crawford said later. "It's an arrogance thing. We don't think of the bad that can happen."[25] Right after the fall, he had a seizure. He spent a week in an intensive care unit, with severe headaches and periods of unconsciousness. He has permanently lost his senses of taste and smell.

Traumatic brain injury (TBI) is the most severe of all skateboarding injuries. Street skating, especially without a helmet, is the leading cause of falls or collisions that lead to head injuries. In 2009, according to the American Association of Neurological Surgeons, 23,114 people were treated in emergency rooms for head injuries related to skateboarding—14,783 of them were children aged fourteen and younger. Skateboarding ranked eighth overall among sports-related head injuries that year, and fifth in children under fourteen. According to Texas neurosurgeon Michael Webb, the number and severity of skateboarding head injuries is increasing. "Almost 50 percent of skateboarding injuries have at least some component of head injuries to them," he says. "The heights have become higher, the speeds have become faster and as a result of that the injuries are greater and more severe."[26]

OFF THE HOOK

20

The average age of the 30 skateboarders who died in 2012 as a result of skateboarding accidents.

One common type of traumatic brain injury is called a concussion. A concussion occurs when the brain is shaken back and forth within the skull as a result of a blow to the head. Milder concussions can cause headache, dizziness, confusion, nausea and vomiting, temporary memory loss, and brief loss of consciousness. A severe concussion can cause prolonged unconsciousness (coma) and damage to nerves and blood vessels in the brain. Most concussions can be treated with rest and pain medications. The activity that led to the injury should be avoided until a doctor gives consent to return to it. A second concussion before the first one is healed can cause dangerous brain swelling and permanent brain damage.

Another head injury that can happen from a skateboarding fall is a skull fracture. The skull is made up of several bones that contain and protect the brain. Some skull bones, such as the temporal bone above the ears, are thinner and easier to break than others, such as the occipital bone at the back of the head. Skull fractures can be linear (in a line), stellate (star-shaped), or depressed (pushed in). Treatment of a skull fracture depends on the location and severity of the fracture, and whether or not there is any damage to the brain.

Hazards of Street Skating

In December 2013, fourteen-year-old Matthew Skovorodin was riding his longboard in the street near a friend's house. His friend, Anatoliy Volovodik, saw a van coming: "I screamed, 'Car! Car!' but Matthew didn't have time to turn with his longboard,"[27] he said. The van hit Skovorodin from behind, then sped off without checking to see if Skovorodin was injured. Skovorodin was treated at the hospital for a fractured right wrist, a lacerated ear, and scrapes on his legs and back. "I was lucky that time that nothing worse happened,"[28] said Skovorodin.

The great majority of fatal skateboarding injuries occur from being hit by a vehicle while riding in the street. Skateboarders have no protection from vehicle impact. In addition, skateboarders are not always easy for drivers to see, especially at dusk or after dark. Skovorodin's accident happened at 9:30 P.M.

Injuries from vehicle impact range from cuts and scrapes to broken bones, head injuries, and internal injuries. Several skateboarding fatalities occur each year. According to the 2012 USA Skateboarding Fatality Report conducted by Skaters for Public Skateparks, Inc., there were thirty reported deaths of skateboarders in the United States in 2012, down from forty-two in 2011. All thirty were killed in public streets, and all of them were male, including an eight-year-old who was buttboarding down his driveway and rolled into the street. Twenty-four were hit by a vehicle, the rest were from falls.

Another hazard of street skating involves collisions between riders and pedestrians. In July 2011, a seventeen-year-old California longboarder collided with an eighty-three-year-old woman who was crossing the street. She was knocked to the ground and later died of her injuries. Such

Skateboarding in the street can be dangerous as most fatal skateboard injuries involve collisions with cars.

collisions can be avoided by staying off the street whenever possible, being aware of one's surroundings, going slowly and having proper control of the skateboard including knowing how to stop, giving pedestrians the right of way, and getting off the board in crowded areas.

Preventing Skateboarding Injuries

"Skateboarding can be dangerous," says orthopedic surgeon Andrew Peretz, "but there are a lot of things skateboarders can do to prevent injuries and to minimize their severity when they do occur."[29] Skateboarders must take responsibility for their own safety. The two most important things a skateboarder can do are to follow safety guidelines and wear protective equipment.

According to the American Academy of Pediatrics, children under age five should not ride skateboards at all. Children aged six to ten should be closely supervised by an adult whenever they ride a skateboard. Skateboarding is a special risk for young children because they have a higher center of gravity, less muscle development, and poor balance. They are less able to break their falls because they have slower reaction times and less coordination than adults. Children also have less skill and ability than they may think. They may overestimate their skills and abilities, and are inexperienced in judging speed, traffic, and other risks. All these factors make young children more likely to fall and get injured.

Beginners should start learning at a skate park or other location that offers well-qualified trainers to teach the basics. Skills should be practiced regularly, on soft surfaces at first, such as grass, carpet, or mats, until balance and control are developed. Practice should

Adults should closely supervise children between the ages of six and ten while skateboarding.

then take place on smooth paved surfaces where there is no traffic, such as a basketball court or an empty parking lot. Less experienced skateboarders should always be aware of their abilities and take time to learn new tricks.

All riders need to be aware of their surroundings. At skate parks, they should follow the rules of the park and observe proper skate park etiquette. They should be aware of others in order to avoid collisions, and, if traveling in the street is absolutely necessary, they must pay attention to traffic, pedestrians, and obstacles such as curbs, gravel, and potholes. Skateboarders should never hang on to the back of a moving vehicle or bicycle ("skitching") and should avoid riding in the rain or after dark. Mountainboarders should inspect

Young Boarder an Ambassador for Safety

Evan Doherty of Greenwood, Missouri, was just five years old when he began skateboarding competitively, becoming the youngest person to successfully land a 720 (two full midair turns) on a half-pipe. He has won many competitions and has traveled all over the United States.

From the very beginning, his motto has been, "No helmet, no skate." (His first helmet was bright yellow with bees on it!) Today, "Big E," as he has come to be called, is ten and is the spokesman for the Big Safety campaign at the University of Kansas. The campaign aims to inform kids and parents about the dangers of concussions and ways to avoid them. As spokesman for the campaign, Doherty encourages other kids to pledge to always wear a helmet when skateboarding. The hope is that even if kids do not always listen to their parents, maybe they will listen to someone closer in age. Says Doherty, "You can heal your broken arm, but your broken head—not so much."[1]

1. Evan Doherty. "Take Ten." Evanskater.com. http://evanskater.com/index.php /take-ten.

any trail about to be used for large rocks, fallen trees, and other potential hazards before riding it.

Skateboard maintenance is very important. Riders should ensure their boards have no cracks or sharp edges, that the trucks are not too loose or too tight, and that the wheels are in good condition and roll freely. Worn parts should be replaced. Personal maintenance is also important: Skateboarders should eat right and warm up with stretches before riding. Additionally, they should not skate when fatigued or feeling unwell. Avoid toxins such as cigarettes, alcohol, and drugs.

Protective Gear

The single most important piece of protective equipment for skateboarders is a good quality, well-fitting helmet. Head injuries are the most difficult injuries to recover from and can cause concussions, permanent disability, or even death. Skateboarding helmets should meet the ASTM F1492 requirement, which establishes standard levels of construction for skateboarding and trick-skating helmets. (ASTM stands for the American Society for Testing and Materials.) A helmet that meets this standard has foam cushioning on the inside, a strong outer shell that can withstand many impacts, and a sturdy strap to hold it in place. The helmet should fit well enough that it does not move around on the head or interfere with vision or hearing.

Along with the helmet, a good set of elbow pads and knee-pads will help protect the rider's joints from cuts, scrapes, and even broken bones caused by impact with the ground. This type of gear also make falls on vert ramps less likely to cause serious injury. Wrist guards help prevent forearm fractures, the most common fracture among skateboarders. For boys who like to grind rails, a protective cup is also a good idea. Hip pads, skateboard gloves, and padded jackets and shorts all help absorb impact and protect the rider.

Skateboarding is very hard on shoes. The gritty grip tape on the deck that lets the rider control the board wears down shoes very quickly, especially with aerial tricks. (The worn-down places on regular shoes is called "ollie burn"

by boarders.) Special shoes made just for skateboarding have wide, flat, hard-rubber soles for good grip, and tough, thick uppers that resist ollie burn. Good quality, well-fitting skateboard shoes last longer, grip the board better, and support and protect the feet better than regular athletic shoes.

Injuries are an almost unavoidable part of skateboarding, but by following safety recommendations and wearing the right protective gear, the chances of getting injured can be greatly reduced. If an injury happens, however, it is important to follow a doctor's recovery plan, including physical therapy, if necessary, and to be patient when getting back on the board. "Injuries will happen; it's the reality of being an athlete," says skateboarder Knoop. "It's important to approach injuries with patience and figure out what your treatment options are. You don't want to rush it because it's easier to heal right the first time than to deal with a chronic injury that never goes away."[30]

Although accidents are common in skateboarding, wearing the right protective gear reduces the likelihood of sustaining serious injuries.

CHAPTER 6

Skateboarding Culture and Psychology

S kateboarding, as a sport, has produced a unique kind of social culture over the years since it began as an off-shoot of the surfing culture in the 1950s. It is today, and has always been, a sort of fusion, or blend, of the trends, fads, and cultural developments within the larger society around it. The great majority of skaters are under the age of thirty, and, as a result, skateboarding culture has adapted to reflect the cultural styles and attitudes of the youngest members of society in each decade. Unlike any other sport, skateboarding is a constantly changing reflection of the youth culture at any given time. It is not the same today as it was ten years ago, and it will not be the same ten years from now as it is today.

What Skateboarding Means to Skateboarders

If there is one constant in skateboarding, it is in its incon-sistency in what it means to skateboarders. "Skateboarding means something different to just about everybody," says Steve Cave, an avid boarder and skateboarding writer and teacher. "Think about it—you could mean riding a vert ramp, technical tricks in the driveway, riding a longboard across campus, bombing a hill with deep curves, slalom, skate park or anything else you like doing on a board with wheels nailed to the bottom. . . . And here's the thing—it's all *right*. A lot of people throw out the phrase, 'Skateboarding is all about _____,' and I'm sure they mean it. For them, it's true. But what fills that blank is different for each of us."[31]

What skateboarding means to the people who love it is even more than what kind of riding they do. It has many, much deeper meanings as well. For some, it means the thrill, the danger, the risk of trying a new skill or trick and maybe getting hurt. For others, it provides a way to channel negative emotions, such as anger, into something more constructive and positive. For many, it provides a powerful sense of accomplishment, pride, and success when they have pushed themselves and persevered and have finally landed that trick they've been working on for months.

For many skaters, it is all about freedom—the freedom to do whatever they want and know that nothing is wrong about it. "In skateboarding," says skater Oliver Hirama, "there's no rules, there's no goal, there's no limitations. No one's ever going to tell you that you're God or that whatever you're doing is wrong

because it's completely subjective. You decide what to do on your own, based on what you think is cool or what you think would be the most fun. And that's what makes skateboarding so amazing."[32]

There is also another kind of freedom in skateboarding that does not exist in many other sports. Many kids leave organized sports around eleven or twelve because staying in them means they have to move up to a more competitive

A group of skateboarders watch a friend perform tricks at a skate park. For many riders, skateboarding provides a sense of community and friendship.

The International Society of Skateboarding Moms

The International Society of Skateboarding Moms was founded in 2004 by Barbara Odanaka, former sports reporter and author of the children's book *Skateboard Mom*. It started with about fifty members from the United States, Canada, and England, and their goal was just to have fun skating and to do something outside the "Mom" stereotype. Today there are more than three hundred members, from all walks of life, ranging in age from twenty-five to eighty (yes—eighty)! Their mission is to empower women and girls through skateboarding. They are also interested in children's literacy. Every Mother's Day, they put on an event called the "Mighty Mama Skate-o-Rama." The event is a fundraiser for children's library services and is the kickoff event for their literacy program, "Rolling4Reading," which provides needy children with books. The books are delivered by skateboard to the children.

Many of the members skated when they were kids in the 1970s and 1980s; now that they have kids of their own who are skating, the "fever" has struck again! Skating gives them a chance to do something fun with their kids, get exercise, and experience the thrill of skating and learning new tricks, despite the bumps and bruises. Most kids whose moms are members think it is cool, and they enjoy watching their moms and cheering them on.

level. For them, this adds a lot of pressure and takes much of the fun out of it. Skateboarding is not like that. A skateboarder can enjoy riding for years without ever having to enter a competition. The only pressure a skateboarder feels is the pressure he puts on himself to get better.

For many skaters, skateboarding provides a sense of community—a group of friends who encourage and support each other no matter what their background is, what kind of family they come from, how old they are, or how good at it they are. At any skate park, on any given day, there will be skaters from wealthy families and skaters who are homeless. There are skaters of all races, religions, ages, and skill levels. There are no differences—they are all just skaters. There may be countless reasons to skate, but all skaters share two things in common: their love of and devotion to skateboarding. There is no time to be superior to anyone else because it will not last forever.

"We're all a family," says Cave. "Save your hate for something else, focus it into your skating, if you want, ride your way, and enjoy it all. It won't be long before you're too old, or too broken, or skateboarding has evolved and your style has been left in the dust."[33]

The Skateboarding Mindset

The freedom, creativity, and individuality of skateboarding are all important parts of an attitude that characterizes skaters at all levels of talent and skill. Like any sport, the right mindset is critical for anyone wanting to enjoy skateboarding and excel at it. A skateboarding blogger who calls himself "BillytheBanman" writes:

Let's face it, if you don't have the right mindset for skateboarding, it's going to be tough being a skateboarder. It's going to be a constant struggle trying to learn new tricks and it's going to take an enormous amount of confidence for you to even think about landing certain tricks. Having the right attitude is key for skateboarding success. This will give you the ability to land tricks quicker and easier, your style will improve, your confidence will increase, and you will also be able to land tricks more consistently than ever before.[34]

Certain attitudes are important for a skater to adopt. First, he needs to have confidence. He needs to believe that anything is possible and that he can achieve whatever he sets out to do. Second, a skater needs to express his individuality and uniqueness and just be himself, instead of trying to be like anyone else. Third, a skater needs to just relax and have fun with skateboarding and not turn it into a chore or a struggle.

Skaters who adopt these kinds of beliefs are more likely to excel, and even become professional skaters. Even professionals keep these basic attitudes, and adopt others as well. Professional skaters set high goals for themselves and truly believe that they are fully capable of reaching those goals.

They visualize themselves performing their tricks flawlessly and imagining how it feels to succeed. They avoid negative thoughts such as "I couldn't do that" or "I'm afraid to try that." They surround themselves with positive, supportive, inspiring people who project positive attitudes, and they learn and improve from being around better skaters.

Most competitive skateboarders have their own ways of preparing themselves mentally, as well as physically, for competitions. In a 2010 interview with ESPN, when asked how he prepares for competition, pro skater Terry Kennedy said, "Just practice. That's it. Just mentally practice, practice physically, work out and take time just to gather myself and have my mind together when it's time for me to focus and get out there and skate."[35]

Competitive skateboarders, such as Terry Kennedy (seen here at a 2010 event), must prepare mentally as well as physically before a competition.

Canadian pro skater and X Games medalist Pierre Luc Gagnon has a similar approach: "I just go to the ramp every day [and] work on new tricks, work on lines, combos [and] new combinations of tricks. I usually . . . do some [core work] in the morning, then go skate in the afternoon."[36]

Into the Mind of the Skateboarder

Considering that there are millions of skateboarding enthusiasts in the world, there has been relatively little research into the psychology of boarding and boarders. One researcher who has looked into the skateboarder's mind is Mike Boyd, of Cal State Fullerton University. In 2001, he was sitting on a bench at a San Francisco bus station, watching a skateboarder trying to land a jump. At one point, the skateboarder fell and banged himself up pretty badly. A friend ran to him and asked if he was OK. "Yeah, I'm all right," the skateboarder answered. "I've been working on this trick for a year, and I'm going to get it yet."[37]

Boyd, a former high school football coach, became interested in the perseverance of skateboarders, despite the high likelihood of getting hurt, and in spite of the general negative attitude toward skateboarders by much of society. "Skateboarders get a bum rap," says Boyd. "People kick them out of places. These guys never say die. They are like artists. They never give up."[38]

Boyd knew that this kind of perseverance was common in high-level athletes, such as professionals and Olympians, and he wondered if the same character traits present in elite athletes were also present in skateboarders. He measured these traits using a well-known measure of sports psychology called the "Iceberg Profile."

The Iceberg Profile is a nickname given to a psychological measurement tool called the Profile of Mood States (POMS). This tool is popular among sports psychologists for comparing mood characteristics of elite athletes compared to nonathletes. Six mood states are measured: tension, depression, anger, vigor, fatigue, and confusion. Subjects are given a score for each mood state depending on their responses to statements that include key words such as "unhappy,"

Skateboarding Language

Whether you are a newbie, a grom, or a veteran gear-head, it's important to know the lingo of skateboarding so you won't look like a total poser, dude. Says skateboarding writer Tomm Smith:

Skateboarders . . . belong to a niche group. That said, they have a set of terms that only they understand. For one, that sort of language keeps them apart from the others. Aside from that, it also serves a practical purpose. Just like in other groups, having terms that are particular to their group makes talking about skateboarding-related topics easier to discuss.[1]

There are hundreds of slang terms used by skateboarders, not to mention hundreds more names for tricks, and it can be intimidating to listen to skateboarders talk to each other. Some words, such as "gnarly" and "carving," were adopted from surfers. Others, such as "grinding," are unique to skateboarding. Being around skateboarders and listening to how they talk to each other is a good way for a beginner to pick up on the language.

1. Tomm Smith. "Skateboarding Lifestyle." EzineArticles.com. http://ezinearticles .com/?Skateboarding-Lifestyle&id=4380445.

"tense," "careless," and "cheerful." For each statement, subjects rate how they feel at that moment and during the past week, using a scale of 0 (not at all) to 4 (extremely).

Elite athletes from various sports tend to score below average (an average score is 50) for negative states, such as tension, depression, fatigue, and confusion, and score above average on vigor (the ability to persevere in the face of obstacles or setbacks, and to work hard to excel at the sport). When plotted on a line graph, the scores for elite athletes have a characteristic shape that has been called the "iceberg," because of the spike in the middle for the attribute of vigor. Generally, the better the athlete, the higher the spike.

Boyd administered the POMS to sixty-eight skateboarders

in San Francisco. All were male, between the ages of eighteen and twenty-eight. The results of his study, which also included measures of goal-orientation and thrill-seeking behavior, were published in the March 2007 issue of the *Journal of Sport Behavior.* It showed that the most determined, most focused, and most successful skateboarders have mood profiles that closely match those of elite athletes in other sports, with higher scores for vigor and lower scores for the other five mood states. Skateboarders with higher scores for thrill-seeking also had high vigor scores on the POMS.

Risky Business

One of the attractions of skateboarding for many skateboarders is the risk involved. Skateboarding carries with it a relatively high risk of getting hurt, but the risk does not seem to stop its fans. The rush of flying into the air and landing back on the ground or of speeding down a steep hill, the thrill of landing that new trick, the applause of the crowd at a competition— these things are powerful motivators that make the risk of injury worth it for many riders.

For many skateboarders, the rush of flying into the air and performing other tricks is worth the risk of injury.

Several factors affect how much and what kinds of risk-taking a person is willing to do. For example, one's personality can determine whether he chooses extreme sports, or traveling to dangerous places. Cultural influences, such as peer pressure, may motivate people to engage in risky behavior such as smoking cigarettes or driving too fast.

Genetic influences may determine how a person's brain responds to risk-taking. The desire to take risks is thought to be hard-wired into our brains, especially in younger males. This may help explain why most skateboarders are male, especially at elite levels.

Risk-taking causes changes in the brain, including the release of adrenaline, the hormone that causes that rush feeling, and dopamine, a chemical that creates sensations of pleasure. This is important because reasonable risk-taking is beneficial to people in many ways. It allowed ancient humans to hunt and kill wild animals for food, and to move to new places when food became scarce. In the modern world, it helps combat boredom and depression and improves mood. Risk-taking leads people to do big things such as making important new scientific discoveries or starting a new business, or simpler things like crossing a busy street, asking a girl out on a date, or trying that cool new skateboard trick.

Skateboarding Culture

Because, in the beginning, the skateboarding culture was tied to the surfing culture of California, skateboarding adopted much of the slang, dress, music preferences, and attitudes of surfers. As skateboarding spread across the country, however, it began to develop a culture of its own.

During its upsurge in popularity in the 1980s, the skateboarding culture became tied to punk culture, which appealed to skateboarders because of its focus on individual freedom and independent thought. As a result, skateboarding came to be seen as an expression of rebellion. Skateboarders developed a reputation for being social nonconformists, with bad attitudes and little respect for authority. In many places, they were even thought of as criminals or delinquents.

Skater and writer Nan Adie recounts this story:

I worked in a government office a few years back. I was the guy to go to if people needed help with spreadsheets and computer stuff like that. They knew I was good at what I did. Once while working on a special project with an older staff [member] I got a rather weird comment. He asked me, "You are a skateboarder right?" I said, "Yeah!" He replied, "How did you stay out of jail long enough to get this job?" I had no reply. I am pretty sure he was just making jokes with me but it drives home a point. Most people over the age of 40 think of skateboarders as criminals.[39]

Throughout the 1980s and 1990s, many communities passed laws sharply restricting where skaters could skate, or even banning skateboarding altogether, as skateboarders were seen as trespassers who tended to damage private property. Adie admits that this is a real concern. "Skateboarding often damages property," he says.

This is true. Skateboarding leaves marks on some property. . . . Private property owners don't want skaters hanging around. They don't want damage, messes or injuries on their property. When people tell teens to

Skateboarding Music

Like with surfing, from which skateboarding evolved, music is a very important part of the skateboarding culture. Early skateboarders most likely listened to the same kinds of music as surfers. In the 1970s, the Caribbean genre of music called reggae became popular, and its freethinking, antisocial themes made it popular among skateboarders. In the 1980s, as skateboarding became faster and more aggressive, skateboarders wanted music that reflected the newer, edgier styles of riding and attitude. Punk rock and heavy metal became the genres of choice.

Skate punk, also called skate rock or skate core, is a form of punk rock especially popular among skateboarders. The members of many skate punk bands, such as The Big Boys and JFA (Jodie Foster's Army), are skateboarders themselves. Skate punk originally developed in the late 1970s, with the first punk scenes in New York, California,

and London, England. It is now popular among boarders all over the world. At first, skate punk had a raw, aggressive sound, played loud and fast, but in the 1990s it became somewhat more melodic, with more harmonious vocals.

Today, punk and metal are still favorites among skateboarders for their hard-driving beat and edgy lyrics, and most skaters have their favorite bands and songs that get them pumped up. "But that's not to say that the musical tastes of skaters have not evolved over those three decades," says skateboarding writer Tomm Smith. "Today, it's not at all surprising for skaters to listen to hip hop music too. The thumping beats that's typical of this music genre also goes great with skaters who want to pump themselves up when doing tricks."[1]

1. Tomm Smith. "Skateboarding Lifestyle— Skateboarding Music." EzineArticles.com. http://ezine articles.com/?Skateboarding-Lifestyle---Skateboarding -Music&id=4846855.

10%

The estimated percentage of skaters in the United States who are female.

leave they usually get attitude. That's just teens. There are solutions to this problem like providing good places to do the activity.[40]

Today, the skateboarding culture is a blend of all of these past societal influences, from surfing culture to punk and many others. The bad reputation that used to be so common has faded, and skateboarding has become more mainstream and may even be an Olympic sport someday. Says Adie:

This bad reputation is a remnant from the past. Most skaters are no different than any other kids or athletes. They love what they are doing and have fun while doing it. Forget the stereotype, it does not fit any more. The outdated image of skaters as criminals is a thing of the past. Nowadays it is the positive skateboarding attitude that rules. This skateboarding attitude is what makes me happy to be a part of such an interesting crowd as skateboarders.[41]

For true "gearheads" (skateboarding enthusiasts), skateboarding is more than just a hobby or a sport; it is a way of life. For many of them, it represents an instant and close-knit community, almost like a family, of supportive, encouraging, like-minded people to whom they can relate and with whom they can develop meaningful relationships. Skateboarding is a way for skateboarding enthusiasts to express themselves as individuals—through the music they listen to, the clothes they wear, and the language they speak. It is also a way to express their creativity through the look of their boards and the innovative tricks they do with them.

Girls in Skateboarding

Although there have always been female skateboarders, skateboarding has always been a sport dominated by males. During the 1990s, however, with the rise in popularity of skateboarding, more girls got involved. In the early 2000s, female skateboarding stars such as Elissa Steamer,

Cara-Beth Burnside, and Mimi Knoop helped draw more girls into the sport.

Still, skateboarding remains predominantly male. There are several possible reasons for this. In general, girls tend to be less willing to risk injury by skating. Social pressures also discourage girls from skateboarding. Girls may shy away from it because there are so few girls doing it, and they are anxious about encountering negative reactions from the boys at the park. They may also feel self-conscious about skating in front of boys; they may be concerned about not appearing feminine or attractive.

Efforts to attract more girls to skateboarding continue, however. For example, Burnside and Knoop founded the all-female skateboard company Hoopla to encourage female participation. In 2005, Burnside, Knoop, and Drew Mearns

Skateboarding stars such as Mimi Knoop, seen here at the 2008 X Games, inspired more girls to get involved in the sport in the early 2000s.

Marseilles Skate Park is the largest in France and is well known for its brightly painted graffiti.

founded the Action Sports Alliance which, in 2008, helped get equality in prizes at X Games events. Additionally, a documentary called *Underexposed,* by Amelia Brodka, released in February 2014, examines the opportunities for girls in extreme sports, particularly skateboarding, and explores ways to increase those opportunities.

Skateboarding Worldwide

Skateboarding may have originated in the United States, but it certainly grew globally. Skateboarding is now popular in many countries around the world and is gradually gaining in popularity. In many other countries, however, high-quality boards and parts are expensive and difficult to get. There are limited places to skate, with skate parks located mainly in the major cities. Often, the facilities at the parks are not as up-to-date or as safe as in American parks. There are, however, some world-class parks in other countries, such as Black Pearl Skate Park in the Cayman Islands (in the Caribbean). At 62,000 square feet (5,760sq.m), it is the largest outdoor concrete skate park in the world. SMP Skate

Park is the largest park in China at almost 45,000 square feet (4,181sq.m). As France's largest venue, Marseilles Skate Park boasts bowls covered with brightly painted graffiti. Other world-class parks include Stoke Plaza in England and Amazing Square Park in Japan.

One thing that skateboarding has in common, no matter the country, is the sense of community and support shared by skaters everywhere. For skaters, skating is almost like a universal language. Says skater Reuben Najera:

> Seriously, you can travel anywhere in the world and have something in common with people in foreign lands. It doesn't matter where he/she is from or what his/her beliefs are, a kickflip is still a kickflip. It's the coolest thing in the world to be able to connect with others like that. I have played games of "skate" with skateboarders that I can't even have a conversation with due to the language barrier. But we still understand each other through our skateboarding. When one of us would miss or land a trick we knew exactly what was up despite those barriers that would otherwise keep us from communicating.[42]

Professional skater Amelia Brodka adds: "Skateboarding provides all of its participants feelings of freedom, joy, and accomplishment. Being a skateboarder automatically makes you part of a worldwide community of people who cheer each other on and welcome each other into their homes so that you can experience their local skate spots and scenes."[43]

In July 2012, skateboarding actually became a way to help foster peace in the turbulent and war-torn Middle East. Michael Brooke, editor of *Concrete Wave*, a longboarding magazine, got the idea of introducing skateboarding to kids in Israel and the Palestinian territories, countries at the east end of the Mediterranean Sea that have endured decades of military, political, and religious conflict. Modeling his idea after a project called Surfing for Peace, which

OFF THE HOOK
1978–1989

The period during which skateboarding was banned in Norway, the only country to ever ban skateboarding.

OFF THE HOOK

60,000 sq. ft. (5,574sq.m)

The size of Denver Skate Park, the largest in the United States.

brings people together through surfing, Brooke, working along with the Peres Center for Peace in Jaffa, Israel, took thirty skateboards and thirty helmets to the towns of Jaffa and Sderot in Israel and to East Jerusalem in the Palestinian West Bank. Brooke and his team put on a demo show in each town and invited the kids there to experience skateboarding for the first time. All of the kids had lived their entire lives in poverty and under the constant threat of war, but they found pleasure through skateboarding. Many of them did not want the team to leave, and some did not want to return the skateboards!

The experience was also very meaningful for Brooke and his team. "This truly was an amazing experience," says Mickey Kook of Surfing for Peace. "The energy the crew had was unreal. It was filled with unforgettable moments that will last a lifetime."[44]

Tami Hay-Sagiv of the Peres Center adds, "Everyone felt included, both boys and girls, old and young, Hebrew speakers and Arabic speakers. This was an inspiring experience for all of us! It made us all realize again how powerful sport is, especially when you utilize it in the service of peace."[45]

Whether for world peace or just for fun, every skateboarder has his own ideas about what this sport means. Steve Cave says:

> But the great news is that skateboarding is also fun! And not fun like playing a videogame is fun—skateboarding is that deep kind of fun that gets down into your gut. Maybe it's because of all of these other reasons chipping in, plus learning and landing a new trick, feeling the burn and the wind as you fly down the sidewalk, the click-clack sounds and crack of the tail as you ollie, the pull of gravity as you bend your knees and push up a ramp or around a corner—skating rocks![46]

NOTES

Chapter 1: The Story of Skateboarding

1. Quoted in Michael Brooke. *The Concrete Wave: The History of Skateboarding.* Toronto, Ontario: Warwick, 2003, p. 18.
2. Quoted in "The History of Skateboard Culture." http://skateculture history.tripod.com/Scateculture.html.
3. Quoted in "The History of Skateboard Culture."
4. Quoted in Tony Roberts. "To the New Generation of Skateboarders, Frank Nasworthy Is Mr. Wheels." *People*, vol. 6, no. 1, July 3, 1976. www.people.com/people/archive /article/0,,20066642,00.html.
5. Quoted in Roberts. "To the New Generation of Skateboarders."

Chapter 2: The Science of Skateboard Design

6. Quoted in Noel Wanner. "The Science and Art of Skateboard Design." Exploratorium Skateboard Science. www.exploratorium.edu /skateboarding/skatedesign.html.
7. Quoted in Wanner. "The Science and Art of Skateboard Design."
8. Quoted in Wanner. "The Science

and Art of Skateboard Design."
9. Quoted in Brad Jakes. "The Future of Skateboarding." http://ezine articles.com/?The-Future-of-Ska teboarding&id=1618975.

Chapter 3: The Physics of Skateboarding

10. Quoted in Pearl Tesler and Paul Doherty. "Frontside Forces and Fakie Flight: The Physics of Skateboarding Tricks." Exploratorium Skateboard Science. www.explorato rium.edu/skateboarding/trick.html.
11. Quoted in Tesler and Doherty. "Frontside Forces and Fakie Flight."
12. Quoted in "Science of Skateboarding." *Discoveries and Breakthroughs Inside Science*, July 2007. www.ivan hoe.com/science/story/2007/07 /301a.html.
13. Quoted in Nan Adie. "Skateboarding Physics." Skateboardhere.com. www.skateboardhere.com/skate boarding-physics.html.

Chapter 4: Training and Conditioning for Skateboarding

14. Quoted in Jason R. Karp. "Muscle

Fiber Types and Training." Coach
.org. www.coachr.org/fiber.htm.

15. Quoted in Gabe Mirkin. "How
    Muscles Get Stronger." Dr.Mirkin
    .com, May 11, 2013. www.drmirkin
    .com/fitness/2056.html.

16. Quoted in Raginee Edwards. "Bal-
    listic Stretching vs. Static Stretch-
    ing." Livestrong.com, May 10,
    2011. www.livestrong.com/article/4
    38555-ballistic-stretching-vs
    -static-stretching/#ixzz2mQsPeaaq.

17. Quoted in Edwards. "Ballistic
    Stretching vs. Static Stretching."

18. Quoted in Mirkin. "How Muscles
    Get Stronger."

Chapter 5: Skateboarding Injuries

19. Quoted in American Academy of
    Orthopaedic Surgeons. "Skatboard-
    ing Safety." OrthoInfo. http://ortho
    info.aaos.org/topic.cfm?topic
    =A00273.

20. Quoted in Leah Crane. "Skate-
    boarder Mimi Knoop Is Tougher
    than You." GrindTV.com, Decem-
    ber 3, 2013. www.grindtv.com/ac
    tion-sports/skate/post/skateboarder
    -mimi-knoop-is-tougher-than-you.

21. Quoted in Crane. "Skateboarder
    Mimi Knoop is Tougher than You."

22. Quoted in Erin DeSantiago. "Skate-
    board Legend Tony Hawk Injured
    at Downtown Disney 'Skate-
    Jam.'" Examiner.com. www.exam
    iner.com/article/skateboard-leg
    end-tony-hawk-injured-at-dow
    ntown-disney-skate-jam.

23. Quoted in "Report on Injuries
    From Skateboarding in Public
    Skateboard Parks." Judicial Coun-
    cil of California, March 31, 2011.
    www.courts.ca.gov/documents
    /skateboardinjury-parks0311.pdf.

24. Quoted in David Strege. "Bob
    Burnquist Breaks Nose in Nasty
    Fall at X Games." GrindTV.com,
    August 2, 2013. http://www.grind
    tv.com/action-sports/skate/post
    /bob-burnquist-breaks-nose-in
    -nasty-fall-at-x-games

25. Quoted in Kelly Albertelli. "Skate-
    boarding Injury Results in Hospi-
    talization." *Ventura County Star*,
    May 7, 2009. www.vcstar.com/news
    /2009/may/07/skateboarding-in
    jury-results-in-hospitalization.

26. Quoted in Jim Bergamo. "Neuro-
    surgeons Seeing More Severe Skate-
    boarding Injuries." KVUE.com,
    May 12, 2011. www.kvue.com/news
    /Neurosurgeons-are-seeing-more
    -severe-skateboarding-injuries
    -121750639.html.

27. Quoted in Steve McCarron. "Teen
    Hit and Run Victim: 'I was Lucky
    that Nothing Worse Happened.'"
    KPTV-KPDX Broadcasting Cor-
    poration, Portland, Oregon, De-
    cember 13, 2013. www.kptv.com
    /story/24210751/teenage-hit-run
    -victim.

28. Quoted in McCarron. "Teen Hit
    and Run Victim."

29. Quoted in "Preventing Skateboard
    Injuries." HealthNewsDigest.com,
    August 2012. www.somersortho
    .com/somersorthopaedicdoctors

inthenews/preventing-skateboarding-injuries.

30. Quoted in Crane. "Skateboarder Mimi Knoop is Tougher than You."

Chapter 6: Skateboarding Culture and Psychology

31. Quoted in Steve Cave. "What Skateboarding Is All About." About.com. http://skateboard.about.com/od/skateboardinglifestyle/a/WhyILikeSkate.htm.

32. Quoted in Oliver Hirama. "The Physics of Skateboarding." YouTube Video, May 11, 2012. www.youtube.com/watch?v=124xlnA8i9k.

33. Quoted in Cave. "What Skateboarding Is All About."

34. Quoted in BillytheBanman. "Secrets of Skateboarding" blog. September 9, 2013. http://thesecretsofskateboarding.wordpress.com.

35. Quoted in Kelly Carter. "Terry Kennedy Takes Aim at Television." ESPN.com, October 11, 2010. http://sports.espn.go.com/espn/page2/story?id=5675000.

36. Quoted in Matt Siracusa. "Interview with Pro Skater Pierre Luc Gagnon." *Stack*, September 1, 2009. www.stack.com/2009/09/01/interview-with-pro-skater-pierre-luc-gagnon.

37. Quoted in Marla Jo Fisher. "Fullerton Researcher Picks up on the Skateboarding Vibe." *Orange County Register*, July 8, 2007. www.ocregister.com/articles/boyd-71785-skate

boarders-skateboarding.html.

38. Quoted in Fisher. "Fullerton Researcher Picks up on the Skateboarding Vibe."

39. Quoted in Nan Adie. "Skateboarding Attitude Is a Blessing and a Curse." Skateboardherc.com. www.skateboardhere.com/skateboarding-attitude.html

40. Quoted in Adie. "Skateboarding Attitude Is a Blessing and a Curse."

41. Quoted in Adie. "Skateboarding Attitude Is a Blessing and a Curse."

42. Quoted in Reuben Najera. "The Universal Language of Skateboarding." 5ones.com—Profiling the Action Sports Industry, March 24, 2008. http://5ones.com/universal-language-skateboarding-046.

43. Quoted in M.J. Leeds. "'Underexposed' in the Public Eye: Amelia Brodka Interview." Skatepark.org, March 30, 2013. www.skatepark.org/park-development/advocacy/2013/03/underexposed-in-the-public-eye-amelia-brodka-interview.

44. Quoted in Steve Cave. "Skateboarding for Peace in the Middle East." About.com, 2012. http://skateboard.about.com/od/skateboardinglifestyle/a/Skateboarding-For-Peace-In-The-Middle-East.htm.

45. Quoted in Cave. "Skateboarding for Peace in the Middle East."

46. Steve Cave. "Top 6 Reasons to Skateboard." About.com. http://skateboard.about.com/od/skateboardinglifestyle/tp/6ReasonsWhySkat.htm.

air/catching air/getting air: Term to describe when all four wheels are off the ground.

backside: A trick done with the rider's back toward the obstacle or ramp.

carving: Skating in a long, curving arc.

deck: The wooden part of the skateboard on which the skater rides.

dude: A general term used to address people, often both boys and girls.

frontside: A trick done with the rider facing the obstacle or ramp.

gnarly: Bad, disgusting, horrible, ugly, etc.

grinding: Riding an obstacle on one or both sets of trucks, rather than on the wheels.

grip tape: Sandpaper-like material glued to the deck to provide traction.

half-pipe: U-shaped ramp, usually with a flat bottom, for doing vert tricks.

kickflip: A trick in which the rider flips the board 360° along its long axis in midair.

nose: The front of the skateboard.

off the hook: Really cool or awesome.

ollie: A jump performed by "popping" the tail off the ground and raising the board into the air.

pop: To strike the tail against the ground to initiate an ollie or other air trick. Also, a measure of how high off the ground a particular board can get.

poser: A person who really has little skill but acts as if he has a lot.

set: A set of steps or stairs.

shove-it/shuvit: A trick in which the rider turns the board 180° horizontally in midair.

tail: The rear of the skateboard.

trucks: The axle assemblies that connect the wheels to the underside of the deck and allow it to turn.

vert: A style of skating that uses ramps or bowls with vertical surfaces.

Books

Michael Brooke. *The Concrete Wave: The History of Skateboarding.* Toronto, Canada: Warwick, 2003. A history of skateboarding, with features about stars, inventors, companies, etc., as well as personal stories from other well-known writers and skaters.

Rebecca Heller and Patty Segovia. *Skater Girl: A Girl's Guide to Skateboarding.* Berkeley, CA: Ulysses, 2007. An introduction to skateboarding for girls who desire to break into the male-dominated sport without fear.

Cole Louison. *The Impossible: Randy Mullen, Ryan Sheckler, and the Fantastic History of Skateboarding.* Guilford, CT: The Lyons, 2011. The history, culture, and major personalities of skateboarding.

Ben Marcus. *Skateboard: The Good, the Rad, and the Gnarly: An Illustrated History.* Minneapolis: MVP, 2011. A highly illustrated story of skateboarding, with contributions from some of skateboarding's biggest stars.

Jocko Weyland. *The Answer Is Never: A Skateboarder's History of the World.* New York: Grove, 2002. Skating journalist and lifelong skater Jocko Weyland tells the story of skateboarding and its culture, including his personal experiences around the world.

Magazines

Concrete Wave, published by Concrete Wave. Billed as "100 percent skateboarding," this publication showcases all forms of skateboarding for skaters of all interests.

Skateboard Mag, published by FlatSpot, Inc. This magazine provides a broad, knowledgeable view of skateboarding culture for all levels of expertise.

Thrasher, published by High Speed Productions. This magazine, which calls itself the "realest, rawest, edgiest magazine on the planet," has been in existence since 1981, highlighting interviews with skateboarding stars.

Transworld Skateboarding, published by Source Interlink. This publication contains skateboarding interviews, contest coverage, features on local scenes, and how-to articles.

Websites

5ones (http://5ones.com/category/skateboarding). This site is devoted to the action sports industry, with a section designated for skateboarding articles, videos, and photos.

About.com—Skateboarding (http://skateboard.about.com). This is a resource that contains links to information about all aspects of skateboarding.

Skateboard-city.com (www.skateboard -city.com). This is a website that serves as an online skateboard community that shares skate videos, skateboard product reviews, tricks and tips, photography, and skateboard industry news.

Skateboarder2.com (http://skateboarder2.com). This site includes links to history, culture, tricks, videos, and other skateboarding sites.

Skatepark.org (www.skatepark.org). This website promotes skateboarding in general and focuses on helping towns get skate parks.

INDEX

A

Aerial tricks, 26, *47*, 50, 57, 86
Angular momentum, 48–50

B

Balance, 59–62, *61*, 69, 84

C

Centripetal force, 50–51, *51*
Chicago Pivot truck, 27–28
Choosing a skateboard, 25, *26*, *33*, 33–35, *35*, 83
   See also individual types of skateboards
Clay wheels, 13, 14, 28
Clothing, 8, 19, 20
Competitions and events
   Action Sports Alliance, 100
   Del Mar Nationals, 15, 17
   Mighty Mama Skate-o-Rama, 90
   mountainboarding, 34
   National Skateboarding
      Championships, 11
   psychological preparation, 92–93
   X/Extreme Games, 19, 20, *45*, 73, 80, 93, *99*, 100
Construction of skateboards, 9, 10–11, 24
Culture of skateboarding, 88–91, 96–98

D

Downhill riding, 16, 21–22, 28, 33–35, 44, 71–72

Dry friction, 44–45, *45*

E

Endurance training, 62–65

F

Falling preparation, 74
Freestyle skating, 16, 18, 35
Friction
   dry friction, 44–45, *45*
   rolling friction, 44
   skateboard tricks and, 45
   static friction, 45
Frontside 180, 48, 49–50, 52

G

Gelfand, Alan "Ollie," 16–17
Girls in skateboarding, 98–100, *99*
Global popularity of skateboarding, 13, 100–102
Gravity, 36, 40–43, 46–47, 49–50
Grip tape, 25, 32, 48, 86

H

Hawk, Tony, 18, 19, *19*, 80
Helmets, 71, 81, 85–86, 102
Hippie jump, 46–47
History of skateboarding, 8–19
Hobie skateboard company, 11, 12
Hydration, 53, 69–70, *70*

PICTURE CREDITS

ABOUT THE AUTHOR

Lizabeth Craig worked for thirty-five years as a registered nurse before leaving the profession in 2013. She began writing as a serious hobby in 2002 and has since published numerous stories and articles for children and adults. In 2007 she began writing for Lucent Books; *Science Behind Sports: Skateboarding* is her twelfth book. She lives in Springfield, Missouri, with her husband, Richard, a cat, and a border collie.

PITT MEADOWS
SECONDARY SCHOOL